For Felicity

ENGLISH ✠ HERITAGE

Book of
Dover Castle
and the Defences of Dover

Jonathan Coad

B.T. Batsford Ltd/English Heritage
London

First published 1995

Typeset by Bernard Cavender Design
Printed and bound in Great Britain by
The Bath Press, Bath

Published by B.T. Batsford Ltd
4 Fitzhardinge Street, London W1H 0AH

A CIP catalogue record for this book is
available from the British Library

ISBN 0 7134 7288 X (cased)
0 7134 7289 8 (limp)

Contents

Illustrations

Colour Plates

Preface and Acknowledgements

Why a book on Dover Castle? The short answer is that no readily-available and reasonably comprehensive history of this important fortress is in print. Moreover, earlier authors such as Darell and Lyon were writing before the immense developments and stirring events of the last two centuries, while more recent authors have tended to concentrate on its medieval history. This book seeks to look at the whole extraordinary story of Dover Castle. In so doing, it is impossible to ignore the fortifications of Dover as a whole, without giving a lopsided account of this remarkable frontier town. Hence the title Dover Castle and the Defences of Dover. Although primarily an architectural history, mention is made of the wider political events which made their mark on Dover. In particular, the momentous struggles here in 1216 and 1940 are described. Then, truly, the castle played a crucial role in national history, justifying its existence and the skills and exertions of the Angevin and Georgian military engineers.

Any author writing about an English medieval royal castle is deeply indebted to *The History of the King's Works*. Other useful sources are also listed at the back. Throughout the years in which I have had the good fortune to be the Inspector of Ancient Monuments responsible for the castle and Western Heights, I have benefited enormously from the experience and help of many individuals. The late Professor Allen Brown made a special study of the castle, mainly for *The History of the King's Works*, partly for the guidebook, and was always a kind and willing sharer of knowledge. Peter Lewis undertook much documentary research on the later history of the fortifications in the 1970s. Wendi Atherton has been especially generous in allowing me to make use of her research on regiments stationed at the castle. The staff of Dover Museum, in particular Christine Waterman and John Iveson, have been unfailingly helpful with their knowledge, as have the staffs of the Public Record Office, Imperial War Museum and the National Maritime Museum. It is also a pleasure to record the help and knowledge of castle staff, especially John Sutton and Steve Carswell, both for long members of the castle conservation team. Without the help of many civilians and ex-service people who served in the castle in the 1939–45 War, it would have been extremely difficult to have presented what I hope is a reasonably balanced picture of events here between 1939 and 1945. 'Hellfire Corner' and this book owe much to them. They are too numerous to mention individually, but an exception must be made for Mary Horsfall, who has indefatigably sought out answers to my numerous questions.

The photographic unit of English Heritage has provided most of the illustrations, many of which were taken by Jonathan Bailey. I am greatly indebted to Dover Museum for figures **2, 17, 42, 44, 45, 48, 51, 52, 54, 56, 60** and colour plates **4** and **13**. The Imperial War Museum provided figures **63, 64, 65, 67**, and **68**; and the College of Heralds figure **13**. Figures **1, 20, 27, 29, 32, 37, 40, 41, 61, 62, 71** were drawn by Kate Morton (copyright Engish Heritage). I owe a special debt of gratitude to Terry Ball for his new, superb reconstruction drawings of aspects of the castle, the copyright for which is held by him.

To all, I am deeply grateful – I hope that they and others will forgive any errors in the text and will find new facts to interest them.

Salehurst, October 1994

Introduction

In the dawn light of 4 June 1940, watchers on the ramparts of Henry II's great keep at Dover Castle saw below them the last units of the Royal Navy and merchant marine entering Dover harbour after their final dash to the mole and beaches of Dunkirk. South of the keep, in Napoleonic tunnels deep in the chalk cliffs, Vice-Admiral Ramsay and his staff were completing an operation which few a fortnight before had believed possible. In the course of nine days, the whole of the British Expeditionary Force, together with French and Belgian troops had been snatched to safety from the encircling German army. The major credit for this extraordinary feat rightly was given to the Admiral and his staff; in providing the locus, Dover Castle once again lived up to its medieval title of the 'key to England'. For the next four years, Dover was once again a great frontier fortress, with an implacable enemy not only across but also in and over the Straits.

At the time of the Dunkirk evacuation, Dover Castle was nearly 800 years old, 900 if we count the castle, little trace of which has been found, hastily erected by William the Conqueror soon after the Battle of Hastings in the autumn of 1066. If, as seems probable, the medieval castle owes its curious shape to pre-existing earthworks of an Iron Age hillfort (**1**), then this hill-top has been fortified for some 2000 years.

Castle and town owe their existence to their geographical location as the point in England nearest to mainland Europe. Here, the shallow valley of the River Dour reaches the sea, making the only break in some 13 miles (21km) of high chalk cliffs. For the first sea-going craft, the river mouth provided a sufficent haven on a stretch of coast notably lacking such facilities. This, together with proximity to France, ensured that Dover was the natural landfall for craft anxious to make the shortest possible crossing of what can be a very rough strait. In 1992, the discovery of the almost-intact remains of a sizeable Bronze Age boat deep in the peaty soil near the old river mouth, points to such cross-Channel traffic having existed for at least 3000 years.

If supposition is correct, the first defence work on the site of the castle was a tribal effort. We have no means of knowing how long the Iron Age hillfort remained in use, or even if it had been abandoned by the time of the Roman invasions. During his first expedition in the summer of 55 BC, Caesar lay off shore at Dover observing the Britons gathering on the heights. Prudently, he chose to land elsewhere. Whether he saw an occupied hillfort on the cliffs, or whether it was just the sheer scale of the latter giving the local forces an advantage, we do not know. In Caesar's second invasion the following year, only one Kentish hillfort offered any resistance. This has been identified

1 *Plan of Dover Castle.*

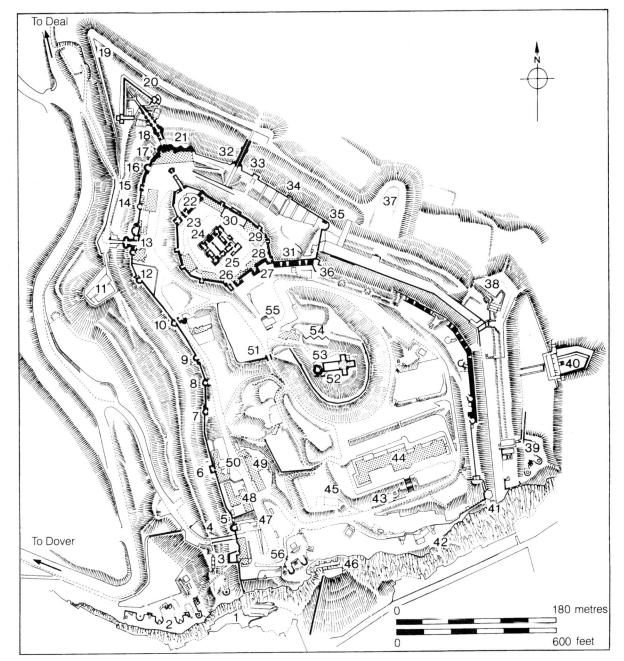

To Deal

To Dover

N

0   180 metres

0   600 feet

KEY
1   Moat's Bulwark
2   Shoulder of Mutton Battery
3   Tudor Bulwark
4   Canon's Gateway
5   Rokesley's Tower
6   Fulbert of Dover's Tower
7   Hurst's Tower
8   Say's Tower
9   Gatton's Tower
10 Peverell's Tower
11 Constable's Bastion
12 Queen Mary's Tower
13 Constable's Gateway
14 Treasurer's Tower
15 Godsfoe's Tower

16 Crevecoeur's Tower
17 Norfolk Towers
18 St John's Tower
19 Spur
20 Redan
21 Underground Works
22 King's Gate Barbican
23 King's Gateway
24 Keep
25 Inner Bailey
26 Palace Gateway
27 Arthur's Gateway, site of
28 Keep Yard barracks
29 Arthur's Hall
30 Keep Yard Barracks
     (regimental museum)

31 Bell Battery
32 Fitzwilliam Gateway
33 Mural towers
34 Mural towers
35 Avranches Tower
36 Pencester's Tower
37 Horseshoe Bastion
38 Hudson's Bastion
39 East Demi-Bastion
40 East Arrow Bastion
41 Site of radar
42 Admiralty look-out/port
     war signal station
43 Stairs to cliff casemates
44 Officers' new
     barracks/Officers' Mess

45 Long Gun Magazine
46 Cliff casemates barracks
47 Powder magazine
48 Royal Garrison
     Artillery barracks
49 Regimental Institute
50 Cinque Ports' prison
51 Colton's Gateway
52 Roman lighthouse
     or *pharos*
53 St Mary-in-Castro
54 Four-gun battery
55 Well
56 Shot-Yard battery

13

as probably being Bigbury, just west of Canterbury. There is no mention of Dover.

Dover's position however was strategically too important for the Romans to ignore. The Roman town of Dubris, from the British Dubra, meaning waters or a stream, was established on the western side of the river mouth in the second half of the first century AD. From the first, it was a trading community, its wealth dependent on its harbour, the importance of the latter attested by the two great Roman lighthouses on top of the flanking hills. This was the *Novus Portus* or New Port mentioned by Ptolemy. In the second century AD the Romans constructed a fort beside the harbour, which became one of the major bases of the *Classis Britannica*, the Roman fleet charged with protecting the Straits and the waters around Roman Britain. When this fleet moved to Scotland in AD 208 the fort apparently was abandoned. Later in the third century, the north-east quarter of this fort was overlain by the construction of one of the much larger Saxon Shore Forts. When this fort in its turn was abandoned with the ending of Roman rule, Dover was left undefended. Very little is known about it between the fifth and seventh

centuries, but its location, together with the extensive pagan cemetery recently discovered at nearby Buckland, indicate that some form of settlement remained and that commerce of a kind continued across the Straits and along the coast.

When Dover re-emerges into written records at the time of the Norman Conquest, its defences have returned to the cliff-top where Caesar first viewed the Britons. Although there was to be a medieval town wall and then from the sixteenth century onwards, harbour defences, the main fortifications have remained on the high ground ever since.

In contrast to the tribal hillfort, from the Roman period successive fortifications here tended to be part of a wider defence strategy. Dover was a small but important cog in the defence and trading mechanism of Imperial Rome. In late Saxon England its fortified settlement formed part of a regional defence system. From the Norman Conquest, with England a unified kingdom, the defences of Dover became and remained the concern of successive governments. There could be no clearer indication of their national importance than this.

1

Settlement and early defences on Castle Hill

The castle which has for so long dominated town and harbour is essentially medieval in plan and silhouette, with major alterations and additions from the mid-eighteenth to the mid-twentieth centuries (**2, colour plate 1**). Its overall shape gives a strong clue to the first defences on this site, while within its colossal earthworks stand the Roman lighthouse, or *pharos*, and the late Saxon church of St Mary-in-Castro, mute witnesses to other occupations here(**3**). From the late twelfth century onwards, the great series of state archives gives us a remarkably detailed account of the develop-

ment of the castle, but for early periods there is virtually no such help. For the period around the Norman Conquest of 1066 we are dependent on one or two enigmatic entries in the records of early chroniclers and on a small number of limited excavations, in advance of conservation works, carried out in the last 40 years. These have shed light on the area of the Inner

2 *A somewhat romanticised view of the castle from the north west by Henry Gastineau, probably painted in the 1820s. The artist almost certainly exaggerates the ruinous appearance of the castle at that time.*

3 *The heavily restored tenth-century church of St Mary-in-Castro stands adjacent to the first-century Roman lighthouse. For much of its early life, the church lay among houses.*

Ward and a small area south of St Mary-in-Castro, but with the exception of the latter excavation, little information has been gleaned on the long pre-Conquest history of the site. But so massive has been the scale of reforming and extending the earthworks from 1750 to roughly 1815, that it is possible that much of the early evidence on the site has been either destroyed or heavily disturbed.

For the presumed Iron Age origins of the defences here we are dependent on the chance discovery of sherds of contemporary pottery – not in itself conclusive evidence given its widespread distribution – and the unusual shape of the ground plan of the castle. Ignoring the Spur earthworks, which were grafted onto the

northern tip of the castle only in the thirteenth century, the irregular outline of the castle's defences is unusual for a major medieval fortification. In part, the shape is dictated by use of the cliff to form an impregnable southern boundary. However, once that is taken into account, if the medieval military engineers had been faced with a comparatively open downland site, they would almost certainly have laid-out a more regular defence plan. Instead, we have a castle whose outer defences are of a decidedly irregular shape, narrowing to a blunt-nosed, somewhat lopsided northern point and with an unusual – in medieval military terms – overlapping of the bank and ditch on the eastern side.

This ground plan can most easily be explained by assuming that the first defences here were an Iron Age hillfort with a single bank and ditch, laid out to follow the contours of the site. Such hillforts were common across the higher ground in southern England in the half-millennium BC The overlapping bank on the eastern side, later to be protected by the multi-angular Avranches Tower (see **15**), could have been the main in-turned entrance to the hillfort.

Such a hypothesis is difficult to prove, but there is nothing inherently improbable about it. The strategic and commercial value of the little haven in the gap in the cliffs would have made its defence as important to the first inhabitants and traders here as it was to be to later generations. Whether the hillfort ever developed its own permanent community or whether it was simply a shelter in times of trouble we may never know.

In the early years of the Roman occupation of Britain, Richborough appears to have been the main entry-point for troops, officials and supplies arriving in the province. But the construction in the second century AD beside the estuary of the Dour of a fort which was clearly associated with the British fleet – the *Classis Britannica* – is strong evidence that Richborough's importance was being challenged by Dover.

The *Classis Britannica* fort is known only from excavations; within the castle however, stands the contemporary *pharos* or lighthouse. This remarkable octagonal tower, its top altered and heightened by Humphrey Duke of Gloucester between 1415 and 1437, was once one of a pair. The second *pharos* stood on the Western Heights, but only part of its base remains, preserved by Georgian military engineers within the Drop Redoubt. These two lighthouses were clearly intended to act as beacons, guiding shipping across the Straits to Dover. Tacitus early in the second century AD mentions the existence of regular cross-Channel traffic.The Dover lighthouses were paralleled at Boulogne by the now-demolished Tour d'Odre.

We know little about the method of operation of these Roman lighthouses, while the medieval alterations of the *pharos* within the castle have destroyed evidence for the original design of the top. We must presume that the two Dover lighthouses acted as sea-marks in fine weather, guiding shipping to the haven which lay between them at the foot of the cliffs. At night fires in braziers in the tops of the lighthouses would have provided beacons of light, welcome sights for mariners on what can be a perilous crossing. To modern eyes accustomed to a super-abundance of electric lighting, a burning brazier may not seem to provide much illumination. But the lighthouses were constructed in a world which knew only the flickering light of a cresset lamp, and where outdoor lighting was unknown. Dusk meant just that; moonless nights were totally dark. In such a world, on such a dark coast with few if any other lights showing, the fires in the tops of the lighthouses would have been visible from a very long distance.

It is possible that the lighthouses were also used as smoke beacons. In certain conditions of weather and visibility, columns of smoke, produced by burning damp fuel, could have augmented the use of the lighthouses as sea-marks. Although there is no evidence, it is not beyond the bounds of possibility that in clear conditions, the Dover lighthouses could have been used as primitive signal towers, linking across the Straits to their Boulogne counterpart or to watchers on the cliffs at Cap Griz Nez.

The immediate surroundings of the *pharos* within the castle, and especially across the valley at Drop Redoubt, have been so altered over the centuries that it is unlikely that substantial traces of any associated structures will ever be discovered. Did the lighthouse keepers live in quarters alongside the lighthouse or, like naval personnel manning the Admiralty tunnels here in the early years of the Second World War, did they climb the hill to work and return to the fleshpots of the town below at the end of their shifts? Whatever the manning arrangements, it is unlikely that they survived the withdrawal of Roman rule in the early fifth century.

A great deal is still unclear about post-Roman Dover. Evidence for fifth century occupation of the site of the town is sparse, but archaeological discoveries show that from the seventh century onwards the heart of the present town was lived in continuously. The establishment of a mint here in the tenth century, probably in the reign of Athelstan (924–39), is the earliest and best evidence for a sizeable urban community. The Domesday survey of 1086 tells us that Dover was already a borough before 1066, able to provide Edward the Confessor with 20 ships, each with a crew of 21, for up to 15 days each year. By then, it was the head-port for a group of south-east coastal towns all providing ship-service for the late Saxon kings – the origins of the Cinque Ports. Given Dover's position, it is highly probable that there has always been some form of community here from Roman times onwards.

It would be rash to make similar presumptions about occupation on Castle hill. Here, waterless upland slopes would have been much less attractive to permanent civilian settlement compared to the comparatively sheltered river banks in the valley below. However, early in the seventh century it is recorded that Edbald, King of Kent, founded a church for 20 secular canons in the castle of Dover. It is possible that castle in this instance may have meant the old Saxon Shore fort; equally it could have meant within the presumed Iron Age ramparts. There are two further pointers towards the latter. First, at the end of the seventh century a successor King of Kent, Wihtred, moved the community to St Martin's church. As this lies within the confines of the Saxon Shore Fort, it would imply that the community previously had been located elsewhere, most probably on Castle Hill.

Then there is the solid evidence provided by the late tenth- or early eleventh-century church of St Mary-in-Castro on Castle Hill itself. Although there is nothing in the surviving fabric of this building which would suggest that it was earlier than the latter part of the tenth century, excavations to the south of it in the 1960s revealed an extensive late Saxon cemetery associated with the church site. The number of burials, which included women and children, implies a much longer occupation here than is suggested by the existing church. Perhaps this is the clearest evidence we shall have that this was the site of a late Saxon defensive work, or burgh, the inhabitants of Dover creating a protected settlement within the Iron Age ramparts above their town in the early troubled years of the eleventh century. Did they see this as a new and permanent settlement, a kind of Upper Town, and build the church to be its heart? Such would seem to be the implication in the Anglo-Saxon Chronicle entry for 1051 (E version), which records the fatal brawling between Eustace and his men who went *up* to the town and slew more than twenty of the townsmen.

Alternatively, was the church already in existence, served by its own community of canons, who found themselves the focal point of a frightened population temporarily intent on using and augmenting the protection afforded by the old Iron Age ramparts? Frustratingly, the various chronicles are silent on these points, but the cemetery here is mute but powerful evidence in support of a more permanent community.

2

The first Dover Castle

In the early autumn of 1066, William's victorious army, fresh from its defeat of Harold at the Battle of Hastings, marched eastwards as part of an encircling move on London (**4**). From Romney, the Duke's forces advanced on Dover, which speedily surrendered. The chroniclers record that William spent eight days here building fortifications before moving on to Canterbury later in November. Nothing of the Conqueror's work survives above ground. What did he find when he arrived and what were the fortifications over which he and his troops laboured for eight days?

One of the key factors in the Normans' rapid conquest and subjugation of England was their introduction of the castle. A very select number of castles immediately pre-date 1066. Three of these are in Herefordshire: Hereford itself, Ewyas Harold and Richard's Castle; one, less certainly, is in Essex at Clavering. These all appear to have been built by Norman or French lords who had settled in England at the express invitation of Edward the Confessor; they are thus Norman transplants rather than indigenous creations.

Dover, too, has frequently appeared on this select list. This story originates with the Chronicler William of Poitier's statement that in 1064 Harold promised Duke William Dover Castle (*castrum Doveram*) when he swore his famous oath to support William's bid for the English throne when Edward the Confessor died. Eadmer, the monk-chronicler writing at Canterbury some 40 years after the events of the Conquest, related that Harold promised to make a castle (*castellum*) with a well at Dover for William's use. He does not mention if Harold kept his bargain, but other chroniclers, some copying one from another, also refer to a castle at Dover, implying that one was in being before the autumn of 1066.

Although firm evidence one way or the other is lacking, it seems more probable that the words *castrum* and *castellum* were being used loosely by the chroniclers to refer to the existing Iron Age hillfort with its possible Anglo-Saxon modifications. These defences would have dominated the sky-line above the river mouth and little town just as the medieval castle does today. Chroniclers recording events here would surely have known of these great earthworks, so much part of the local scene, but would have been ignorant and untroubled by the precise definitions used by much later generations of writers on military fortifications.

Although the size of the Anglo-Saxon defences here is unknown, they would probably have taken the form of a ditched and banked enclosure protecting whatever settlement was centred on the church with its community of canons. Such defences would have been readily adaptable by the Normans. It is unlikely that the Anglo-Saxon inhabitants, and certainly not the much smaller Norman garrison, would have been able to man the vast circuit of Iron Age ramparts. The Anglo-Saxon

4 *An eighteenth-century view of the keep and inner bailey from the north. King's Gate and its protective barbican are prominent in the foreground.*

defences may have been a simple bank and ditch cutting-off some of the southern part of the Iron Age fort. The eight days which William and his forces spent here would have been sufficent to construct only a small defence work within existing fortifications, just as the Conqueror had done a few weeks earlier within the Roman walls at Pevensey.

Depending on what William found here, the time may have been spent simply modifying and strengthening an existing defence work – perhaps by heightening the banks or improving the entrances. The excavations south of St Mary-in-Castro between 1961 and 1963 lend support to the theory of a small defensive work or castle being thrown up within pre-existing fortifications. Here, underneath the great

thirteenth-century bank was found another bank and ditch, some 27ft (8.2m) wide and 18ft (5.5m) deep. Dated to the middle years of the eleventh century, it could have related either to burgh defences or to presumed works by Harold in 1064, or to William's campaign in 1066. As the late Professor Allen Brown wrote: 'Yet the fact that it cut through and disturbed the cemetery, and pressed hard against the south wall of the south transept of the pre-existing church, argues against the first two possibilities, and in favour of the third, whose context is the irreverent urgency of war.'

Although probably incapable of proof, this is an attractive explanation. An invading army intent on securing its bases would have had far fewer scruples than local people about desecrating a cemetery and by implication incorporating a major church into a defensive scheme.

This first brief building campaign though is highly unlikely to have been the only one undertaken here by the Normans in the eleventh century. It must be seen as a temporary measure, the work of an invading army intent on securing its lines of communication. Once the immediate military objective – in this case the surrender of London – had been achieved, time could be devoted to consolidating the more important strategic fortifications, of which Dover Castle was almost certainly one.

This analogy raises intriguing questions about the topography of this part of Castle Hill and the development of the castle between 1066 and the 1180s. Since the 1180s, Henry II's massive keep has dominated the castle and formed its heart and focal point (**colour plate 3**). But the implications of the great ditch found in the 1960s excavations are that the centre of the early Norman defences probably focussed on the area around the Anglo-Saxon church, and on the still-substantial remains of the Roman *pharos*. The massive walls of the former clearly had defensive possibilites in an emergency, while the height of the latter would have been equally useful to a garrison intent on dominating any besiegers.

Extensive alterations to the ground levels here, first by Henry III's engineers and then by Georgian military engineers, make it extremely difficult to envisage the topography of this part of the site as it might have been in 1066. There is however an attractive logic in centring first Anglo-Saxon defences and then the Norman castle on St Mary-in-Castro. Could the existing earthworks of the inner ward and those around St Mary-in-Castro have evolved from an early Norman castle with a motte in the 'waist' between the two (see **1**), as can still be seen at Windsor Castle? This would have left the bulk of the area encompassed by the Iron Age ramparts available for future development. When Henry II's engineers came to remodel the defences, they could build in the northern of the existing wards, leaving most of the existing fortifications intact until the new work was nearing completion, while at the same time gaining additional protection from the prehistoric defences. By this same logic, the present massive Henry III earthwork south of the church, overlying the eleventh-century ditch, represents the redevelopment of the southern part of the castle once its heart had been relocated to the north.

Whatever form William's new castle took, it was soon proving its worth. In March 1067, King William returned on a visit to Normandy. He left England in the charge of his half-brother Odo, bishop of Bayeux and William fitz Osbern. Odo established his headquarters at Dover specifically to guard the Kentish ports and keep open communications with Normandy. But while the bishop and many of his knights were beyond London suppressing unrest, a serious rebellion broke out in Kent. The rebels invited Count Eustace of Boulogne to be their leader. Although a valiant supporter of William at the Battle of Hastings, the count had subsequently quarrelled with the king. Landing at Dover with the aim of seizing both the port and the castle, Eustace attacked the latter before promised reinforcements could arrive. The garrison beat-off the attack, the rebellion collapsed and Eustace sailed back to his country. The necessity for a strong, well-garrisoned castle under the close control of the crown to guard this vulnerable corner of England could not have been more fittingly demonstrated.

No records survive to tell us what works, if any, bishop Odo carried out on the castle before his fall from grace in 1082. Indeed, the records are silent throughout the reigns of William II and Henry I. It is however inconceivable that nothing was done in the century after 1066 to maintain and strengthen what originally can have been only a chalk and earthwork castle. If stone was used for the defences or for the buildings for the garrison and was reused in later construction, it has yet to be identified. Two detached towers which stood in the outer bailey until they were demolished in the eighteenth century, were said to be Norman in origin. Unfortunately, no detailed illustrations of them appear to survive. Their location however, could strengthen the case for the heart of the first castle being centred on the area around St Mary-in-Castro.

However, the tremendous expansion and rebuilding commissioned by Henry II from the late 1160s to the end of his reign points not just to the strategic importance of the castle but also suggests that what existed in the 1160s was both old-fashioned and inadequate. Only wholesale renewal on a positively heroic scale was felt to be a suitable response.

3

The most powerful fortress
in Western Europe

For 34 years from 1154, Henry II ruled an empire which stretched from the borders of Scotland to the Pyrenees. For most of his reign, his boundless energies were concentrated on consolidating and expanding his continental possessions. From the first, he was an enthusiastic builder. As early as 1161, the Abbot of Mont St Michel noted that, 'not only in Normandy, but also in England, the Duchy of Aquitaine, in the County of Anjou, in Maine and Touraine, he either repaired old castles and palaces or built new ones'. In England alone, the royal accounts record Henry spending money on no less than 90 fortifications.

The bulk of the sums expended on individual castles were measured in hundreds of pounds. Five castles had between £1000 and £2000 spent on them; these were at Newcastle upon Tyne, Orford, Winchester, Windsor and Nottingham. In sharp distinction, Dover Castle had a recorded expenditure of £6440. This was an enormous sum, representing a sizable proportion of Henry's income. Major work at Dover continued through the reigns of Richard I and John, giving a final total here of some £8250, more than twice as much as Richard I had spent on the Tower of London.

The most obvious question to be asked in the light of this enormous expenditure is: why Dover? The answer has to be the conspicuous one of Dover's geographical location. Further west, the nearest part of the continent to the southern coast of England comfortingly was

part of the same Anglo-Norman empire. The tip of Kent however, faced across the Straits to the lands of the Count of Flanders, by the later twelfth century a dependent of the King of France. Dover was very much a frontier castle. More than that, in an age which recognised castles as powerful symbols of feudal authority, Henry no doubt felt impelled to build on a grand scale here, to make a positive statement highly visible to shipping using the Straits.

Work at Dover began comparatively modestly. In the 1160s and 1170s total expenditure here was around £500, which suggests that the king's officials were making piecemeal additions to existing defences rather than undertaking a radical reorganisation and strengthening of the castle. It was the ten years 1179–88 which witnessed the spending of nearly £6000 and the construction of much of the medieval castle which survives today (5). This work was largely supervised by Maurice 'the Ingeniator', perhaps best translated as Maurice the Military Engineer, one of the king's trusted officials who had recently been employed on the construction of the new keep at Newcastle upon Tyne.

Maurice's memorial is the great keep (6), the walls of the inner bailey and the north eastern sector of the outer curtain running north from Avranches Tower. This building campaign was to transform Dover Castle, ultimately making it the first castle in western Europe with concentric defences and one of the most powerful

5 *The northern end of the castle. The old north gateway, infilled with the beaked tower after the siege of 1216–17, is in the centre of the view. Just visible below it is the circular top of St John's Tower. This pre-1914 photograph shows the keep without its central crenellations. These were removed* c.*1800 to allow heavy guns on the roof a clear field of fire.*

fortresses of its age. If Maurice, as seems probable, originated the idea of concentric lines of defence – certainly being applied to a medieval castle for the first time at Dover while he was in charge of construction here – he should be ranked among the foremost military engineers of the Middle Ages.

Documentary sources do not tell us precisely how the money was spent on the castle, but excavations just south of the inner ward in 1964 perhaps give us a clue to a possible construction sequence and suggest the form of the defences existing here by the late 1160s. Until destroyed by Georgian military engineers in the last decade of the eighteenth century, there

6 *The north and west faces of the keep. The windows are mostly copies of fifteenth-century replacements.*

existed south of the present inner bailey walls the remains of the medieval south barbican centred on Palace Gate. The essence of a barbican was to provide additional protection to a gateway usually, as here, by forming a right-angled defensible approach to it. Apart from anything else, this arrangement largely thwarted assault by battering ram. Eighteenth century plans show that just near its south-east angle, immediately underneath the existing approach road to Palace Gate, there stood a massive square tower known as the Well Tower (see **6**). The main approach to the barbican was from the east through Arthur's Gate, somewhat awkwardly jammed against the south-eastern tower of the inner bailey. Later in the thirteenth century, as the eastern outer curtain was completed under Henry III, Pencester's Tower was adapted to form the eastern outer entrance to this barbican.

Compared to the northern barbican, whose outer walls continue the curve of the curtain giving it a sense of unity with the inner bailey, the plan of the southern barbican suggests either that it was something of an afterthought or that Henry II's engineers in the 1170s and 1180s had to contend with existing structures in this area. The excavations begun in 1964, limited though they were, pointed to a complex development of the defences here. The excavators uncovered part of the base of a hitherto unknown tower just north of Arthur's Gate. This tower, which was not apparently linked to any curtain wall, was earlier than the towers of the adjacent inner curtain. It had been demolished when the south east angle tower of the inner bailey was extended soon after initial completion. The masonry of the demolished tower, and pottery found associated with it, all point to it being the work of Henry II, possibly the northern half of an early gateway. The absence of any signs of a curtain wall linked to it, and the nature of the footings of the adjacent central tower of the south side of the inner curtain, suggested to the excavators that the area of the South Barbican was once part of the

inner bailey and that this had initially been an earthern enclosure with isolated towers set into the banks. Well Tower was possibly another of these towers.

The dating of this presumed earthwork enclosure at present hinges entirely on the dating of the demolished tower north of Arthur's Gate. Assuming that bank and towers are contemporary suggests sometime early in the reign of Henry II – perhaps in the early 1170s when there is an increase in expenditure over several years. Equally, the towers could have been inserted in an earlier bank, pehaps part of the post-Conquest earthworks. But whatever the extent and nature of the works, they were to be entirely superceded by the remodelling under Maurice.

What is now the heart of the castle was for a decade a vast building site centred on the construction of the keep and the inner and outer curtains. The site provided chalk and flint, but all other materials came from elsewhere. Records mention the carriage of lime from Gravesend, while the walls and keep contain vast quantities of Kentish ragstone. Caen stone from Normandy was used for much of the ashlars and the finer detail. The bulk of materials would have arrived by ship before finishing their journey up the steep castle hill in carts.

Limited evidence, mainly that of the monkish chronicler of St Mary's Priory Dover, suggests that the keep was built before the walls of the inner curtain. This would certainly be logical, avoiding all the problems of keep construction traffic having to struggle through King's Gate and Palace Gate. But it is also likely that work on substantial sections of the inner curtain could have proceeded simultaneously, a course suggested by the results from limited excavations in 1968 in Keep Yard. Gaps, which could be infilled later, could have been left in the curtain and its moat for materials for the keep. Later refacings, and the random nature of the flint and rubble inner curtain, have left no obvious traces of such

7 *The inner ward and keep from the south. The buildings outside Palace Gate, including what is probably the remains of Well Tower, were demolished in the 1790s.*

temporary construction gaps.

Dover keep was the last and most expensive of the great square royal keeps to be constructed, bringing to an end a line which had begun a century earlier with the Tower of London and Colchester. It embodied in their ultimate form most of the features to be found in the major rectangular keeps of the twelfth century (**7**). It stands some 83 ft (25.3m) high; above its plinth it measures 98ft by 96ft (29.9m by 29.3m), excluding its forebuilding. Its walls vary from 17ft to 21ft (5.2m to 6.4m) in thickness and are given added strength by pilaster buttresses in the middle of each face and by clasping buttresses at the corners. These latter rise 12 ft (3.7m) above the main walls to form corner turrets.

Internally there are three floors. The principal entrance is on the top floor, approached by three flights of steps through a massive forebuilding constructed against the south and east sides of the keep (**8**). At the head of the first flight is the lower of two chapels, but before this, a doorway on the left leads to the upper flights. Originally, these two were open to the sky – and to the missiles of defenders behind the battlements above – and were separated by a drawbridge. The ghosts of this may still be seen. At the top of the third flight a guardroom watched over the entrance to the principal floor (**9**).

As with most of the larger English keeps, Dover is divided internally by a cross-wall rising the full height of the building. The thickness of the external walls allowed Maurice to incorporate chambers within them. Some of these were private apartments with their own fireplaces and garderobes; others were garderobes clearly intended for communal use (**10**).

The ground floor was probably always designed for storage and was originally lit only by narrow loops. Here, as elsewhere, there have been many later alterations, but the three large

round headed arches in the cross-wall are original. These must have aided the store-keepers
while lessening the defensive strength of the
building. Linking all floors are wide spiral
stairs in the north-east and south-west corners.

8 *The keep, showing the forebuilding and entrance staircase.
This pre-1914 photograph shows the eighteenth-century
barracks still in use, a loading gantry on the keep wall and
a static water tank on top of the upper chapel roof. Areas of
rendering remain on the keep.*

9 *A cut-away view by Terry Ball of the forebuilding defences.*

10 *Floor plans of Henry II's keep:* **(a)** *basement and ground level;* **(b)** *1st floor and access to level 5;* **(c)** *2nd floor;* **(d)** *mural passages and level 3 (drawn by Terry Ball; copyright English Heritage).*

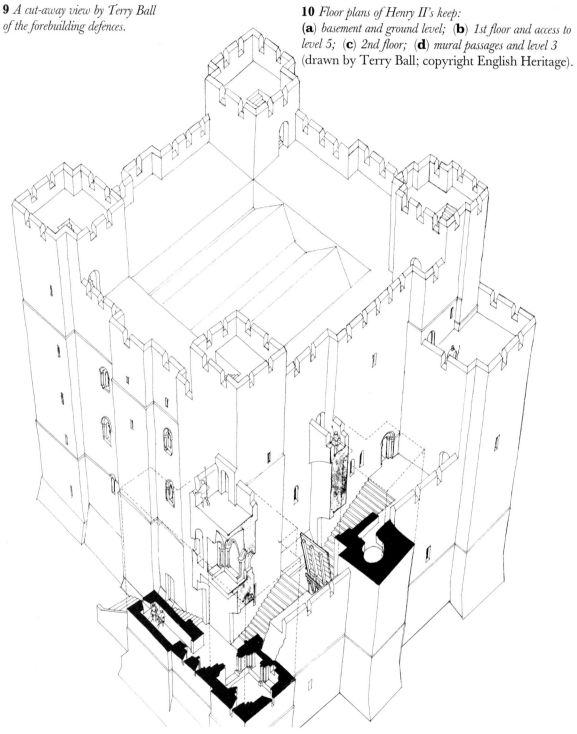

These ascend to emerge in corner turrets at roof level.

The second floor is especially notable for its double height, which allowed for a mural gallery with a second tier of lighting. Alterations, most notably the insertion of the great brick vaults in the 1790s, have led to numerous changes, but it is still possible to

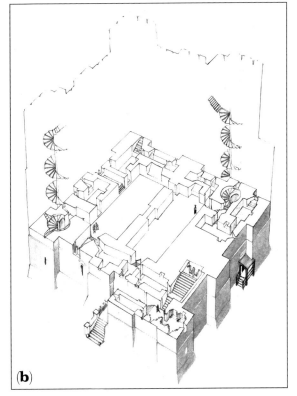

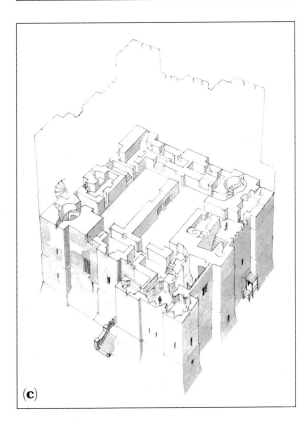

(a)

(b)

(c)

(d)

appreciate the layout of the 1180s. This level was clearly intended as state apartments for use by the king or by important officials (**colour plate 3a**). The spine wall divides the space into two main rooms, lit by tall windows at each end; the present ones are modern copies of fifteenth-century replacement windows. These rooms were no doubt intended to serve as great hall and great chamber. They were linked originally by a doorway in the centre of the wall. This was blocked in the fifteenth century and replaced by the existing central fireplaces and by the doorway at the northern end of the spine wall.

The floor area of this western room is slightly smaller than its eastern counterpart but it is better lit, with a third great window in its western wall. The slender angle shafts with stiff-leafed capitals flanking these window embrasures provide a clue to the richness of the original decorations here. Traces of a twelfth-century stone flue in the west wall indicate the position of the first fireplace. When originally completed, the walls would have been plastered and decorated.

In the thickness of the western outer wall are two roomy chambers, modernised in the fifteenth century. Both are well lit and have their own fireplaces, but the northern chamber also has its own private garderobe and was clearly designed as the king's bedroom, one of the very few places where a medieval monarch could reasonably hope for some privacy (**11**).

In plan and position, the western hall was clearly intended as the king's Great Chamber, a place of private audience for those who had climbed the forebuilding stairs, identified themselves to the guards at the top, and awaited the

11 *One of the chambers in the thickness of the keep walls. This, on the second floor, with its own garderobe as well as fireplace, was almost certainly the royal bedroom.*

royal summons in the outer Great Hall.

This outer hall, or eastern room, is larger than its western counterpart. It, too, is provided with a garderobe, but no trace has been found of a twelfth-century fireplace; the existing one is a fifteenth-century insertion. Unlike the Great Chamber, there are no private rooms contrived in the thickness of the outer walls but in the south east corner a short passage leads to a small chapel with its sacristy (**12**). These occupy the top stage of the south tower of the forebuilding and thus lie directly above the first floor chapel. These are among the least-altered spaces in the keep. The tiny sacristy, which opens off the passage, is lit by two windows and has stone benches around three sides. The chapel itself is twice the size of the one below, allowing for a small ante-chapel or nave. Both sacristy and chapel are notable for the richness of their decoration, the walls distinguished by arcading, the ribs of the vaulting adorned with dog-tooth, the shafts and columns with foliated capitals, and the orders of the archway between nave and chancel separated by deeply undercut chevron ornament. With the vast majority of castle chapels destroyed or fallen into ruin, this upper chapel is a precious survival. It gives an insight into the faith of the age in which it was built. Here, in the heart of a structure built for war, space was found and funds devoted to the glory of God.

The upper chapel was clearly for the use of the king. He could either approach it through the outer of the two main state chambers or, if he wished for greater privacy, he could arrive by means of a wall passage within the south wall of the keep.

The first floor is almost a mirror-image of the floor above. The two main apartments each have their mural chambers and garderobes. Less decoration survives at this level – but there may well have been less originally. The main apartments are only half the height of the apartments above. Unlike the privileged occupants of the floor above, the inhabitants of

12 *The upper chapel in the keep.*

the first floor also had to use the smaller of the two chapels, less conveniently sited across the main thoroughfare of the forebuilding stairs.

This first floor was also modernised in the fifteenth century when doorways, windows and fireplaces were reformed. As with one of their counterparts on the floor above, the main fireplaces here are decorated with carvings of Edward IV's Yorkist badge of the rose *en soleil*. This late fifteenth-century refurbishment also hid the massive timber framing lining the east and west sides of the eastern apartment. This was probably added in the thirteenth century to strengthen the floor above; two centuries later it was encased in brickwork to provide a flush surface to the walls.

The original storerooms, chapels, great chambers and garderobes, private apartments and guard rooms are all readily identifiable 800 years later. What are far less certain are the original kitchen arrangements. Unlike the keep at Castle Rising, which has a kitchen conveniently at one end of the Great Hall adjacent to the Great Chamber of the Albini lords, Dover keep has no space identifiable as a kitchen. During close siege, temporary cooking arrangements could no doubt have been rigged using the fireplaces in the main apartments, but it is unlikely that this was normal practice. More probably, a detached kitchen, isolated to minimise the risk of fire spreading, was built within the inner ward against the curtain wall. The later service arrangements for Arthur's Hall could point to the south-east corner of the

inner bailey as the location of an early kitchen, but this is only surmise. But however close the kitchen to the keep, however fleet of foot the servers struggling up the forebuilding steps, really hot food on the second floor must have been something of a rarity (**13**).

The brick-lined bread oven in the north eastern corner of the basement is almost certainly a fifteenth-century addition. This was probably inserted during the refurbishment of the building,

13 *John Bereblock's 1626 view of the keep and inner bailey from the west. Clearly visible is the pentice or covered walk linking Arthur's Hall to the keep.*

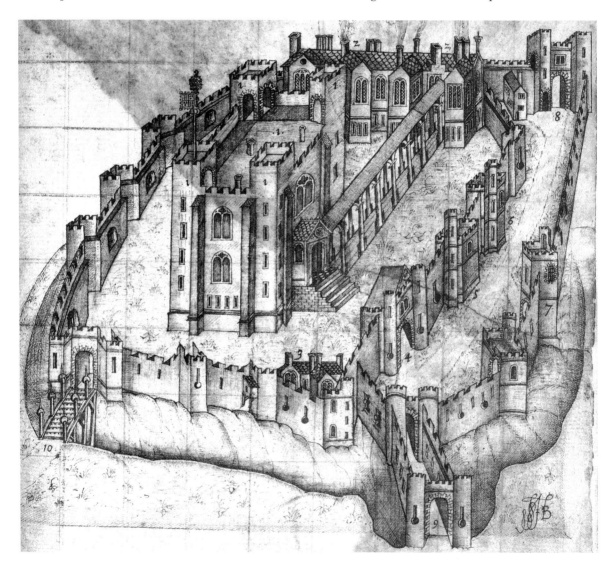

when its perceived role was more becoming more of a grand hotel for itinerant monarchs or their senior officials travelling to and from the continent.

If the whereabouts of the original kitchen are a mystery, the keep's other domestic arrangements, most notably with its water supply, had been well thought out. In a siege, the success of failure of a garrison often turned on its access to food and water. Dover keep follows custom in having its own well, with access only at the second floor in a vaulted well chamber adjacent to the entrance. Cutting this well was a prodigious undertaking as the water table at the foot of the chalk cliffs lies some 400ft (122m) below the keep. For the first 172ft (52m), the well shaft is lined with Caen stone, but the remainder is in the natural chalk. Remarkably, from the well chamber two substantial lead pipes distributed the water by gravity to the two lower floors of the keep. Such elaborate arrangements in the twelfth century were certainly found in the larger monastic houses – Prior Wibert's complex water system at Canterbury was built in the 1150s – but in castles they were extremely rare. The keep at Newcastle upon Tyne has an embryonic system, clearly indicating that the Dover scheme was modelled by Maurice on his earlier work there. At Dover, the well was supplemented by rainwater collected from the roof and piped to a circular stone tank which still survives in part in the middle tower of the forebuilding.

Although primarily for royal accommodation, the keep was also the last stronghold of the garrison if an enemy overran the rest of the castle. Although perhaps most powerful of the twelfth-century English keeps, Dover suffers the same drawbacks inherent in the design of all these monstrous buildings. The rectangular plan led to blind spots at the corners which were also vulnerable to mining. The keep itself was essentially *defensive*. Although it always had looped openings, concentrated fire from these was virtually impossible. Like a medieval war-ship whose armament was largely confined to its main deck, the garrison of Dover keep would have massed their weaponry on the wall-walks behind the battlements.

Dover keep's defensive concept was becoming outdated even before its completion. Early stone keeps had been so strong in comparison to their outer defences that it had not been unrealistic to see them as citadels, capable of independent resistance when the latter had been captured. At Dover, the inner and outer curtains being built at the same time as the keep demonstrated that future fortification design lay in defence in depth, with carefully sited mural towers able to provide cross-fire. The archers on the keep roof, overlooking the outer defences, played a vital part, but the notion that the keep could continue to hold out if all else was lost, must have been becoming increasingly untenable.

The spine wall suggests that Maurice was aware of this shift of emphasis. In origin the spine wall was defensive as well as structural. If a besieging force broke into a keep, the spine wall gave the garrison one last chance of holding out in the other half – as happened at Rochester in 1215. Piercing the spine wall with arches in the basement at Dover made such desperate measures impossible.

Further proof of this change in defensive thinking is provided by the medieval doorway which gives access from Keep Yard directly to the basement, no doubt for the convenience of the storekeeper (see **8**). Although overlooked by archers on the first tower of the forebuilding, and carefully protected by no less than three doors, each with drawbars, this was another significant weakness which would have been unthinkable to earlier keep designers. The construction details suggest that this entrance is an original feature.

Work on the curtain walls first appears in the Sheriff's accounts for 1186, when most of the keep must have been completed. Excavations within the inner bailey between 1957 and 1968 showed that the natural summit

14 *Palace Gate, set between two protecting mural towers. All date from the 1180s, but the gateway was modernised in 1853 and had a new drawbridge installed.*

of the ground here was in the vicinity of Palace Gate and that great quantities of chalk rubble were used to level the area.

The walls of the inner bailey, along with the northern barbican, run roughly parallel to the (presumed Iron Age) outer defences. South west of the keep, the wall bellies out in a great curve, but its north eastern stretch is comparatively straight. At regular intervals there are rectangular mural towers to provide enfilading or cross-fire to protect the curtain. The main gates themselves – Palace Gate to the south (**14**), King's Gate to the north (see **4**) – are sited between two closely spaced towers to give them especial protection. In this, Dover was again setting the pace in the design of what traditionally had always been the weakest part of a castle's defensive circuit. Both gateways were originally protected by barbicans. Although the southern one has long gone, much of the northern one still survives, with its entrance in

the centre, but King's Gate behind it off-set to thwart the rush of an assault party.

The superficially similar mural towers differ significantly in purpose and firepower. Those on the south-west, which was the more exposed side until completion of the outer curtain some 10 to 20 years later, like the gate towers were provided with triple arrow loops on their three outer faces. By contrast, towers along the north-east side only had single loops, though these were supplemented by further loops in the curtain wall. All the towers were open to the rear, but the north eastern towers alone had upper storeys and first floor garderobes built in. Clearly, the straight curtain and towers here were designed to have buildings constructed against their inner faces. Although both curtains and towers lost their battlements in the eighteenth century, they remain outstanding examples of late twelfth-century military architecture.

Although Henry II's building accounts make no specific mention of the outer curtain, the architectural treatment of the length running north east from the site of Penchester's Tower to Avranches Tower and then almost as far as Fitzwilliam Gateway, leaves little doubt that it is the same date. Here are the same rectangular mural towers with battered bases and the same triple arrow-loops grouped under a common arch.

The polygonal Avranches Tower itself is a tour de force, its batteries of arrow loops commanding what was once a causeway where the northern section of the eastern moat overlaps the southern stretch (**15**). Possibly this was once the entrance to the Iron Age hillfort, perhaps re-used by the builders of the first castle. Given this potential weakness, it was no coincidence that it was here that Henry's engineers first began construction of the defences in depth. On completion of Avranches Tower and the adjoining stretches of wall, at least 50 loops in two tiers were able to pour a punishing fire on anyone rash enough to attempt to storm the old causeway (**16**).

15 *Avranches Tower after conservation in the early 1930s; its multiplicity of firing loops is plainly visible.*

16 *The interior of Avranches Tower surveyed by a military engineer in the nineteenth century.*

Henry II died on 6 July 1189, his last year clouded by the revolt of his sons and the alliance of Richard with his old enemy, Philip Augustus, King of France. Initially, Richard I continued the works at Dover, but his heart lay in the Third Crusade and then in construction of one of the most famous of castles, Chateau Gaillard overlooking the Seine. Not surprisingly, expenditure at Dover dropped to a point where it probably only barely covered maintenance costs.

When John succeeded as king in 1199, he inherited a castle rather more than half way through its major transformation. Probably, areas of it were still a giant building site, with raw chalk ditches and piles of materials. The keep was complete, as were the walls and barbicans of the inner bailey, but only a comparatively short length of the outer curtain had been completed on the eastern side. But until this outer circuit of walls was finished, the defences here depended solely on a moat and bank then well over 1200 years old.

Initially, John devoted few funds to Dover. Then in 1204 came the loss of Normandy and Anjou. This dramatic contraction of the Angevin empire focussed the king's attention on his remaining royal fortresses, not least the strategically-vital Dover. A proportion of the renewed expenditure – which was to total nearly £1100 by the time of John's death in 1216 – was spent on domestic accommodation. Archaeological evidence points to construction of buildings within the eastern walls of the inner bailey during this period, while a reference in 1214 to timber from Sussex for a new hall may refer to a building reputed to have stood in the north western part of the outer

17 *Looking south to Peverell's Tower. This rather blurred late nineteenth-century photograph unusually shows guns mounted on this side of the castle.*

bailey. Alone of the towers on this section of curtain, Godsfoe is rectangular, perhaps pointing to its use as a chamber block in association with a hall. In 1207–8, lead was supplied from mines in the Mendips to roof 'houses' in the castle.

The bulk of expenditure must have been devoted to the outer defences. There are few contemporary details, and our best evidence that the works must have been suffcently far advanced to be defensible, comes from the dramatic events of 1216.

In 1205 miners were sent to Dover, probably for digging ditches; this may well mark the resumption of the building campaign on the outer defences. Evidence for progress here comes from the walls themselves and from the known later work of Henry III. John's builders must have resumed construction on the north east side where the works had stopped in 1190. At the northern point of the outer curtain, they sited the main external gateway of the castle, flanked by two towers. The new curtain walls, distinguished by the use of D-shaped rather than the earlier rectangular mural towers, follow the earthworks anti-clockwise round to Peverell's Tower (**17**). From there, a now-vanished length of wall ran north-east to join the defences of the inner bailey near its southern gateway, and thus provide a continuous outer circuit to Penchester's Tower by way of Well

18 *Looking north along the western curtain wall from Hurst's Tower to Peverell's tower.*

Tower, Armourer's Tower and Arthur's Gate.

South of Peverell's Tower the western curtain is the work of Henry III (**18**); probably the eastern curtain south of Penchester's Tower also belongs to his reign. However, Colton's Gateway (**colour plate 4**), and by implication the wall which linked it to Harcourt Tower, was built by John. By 1216, Dover Castle had a double circuit of defensive walls surrounding the keep, but south of Peverell's Tower and Penchester's Tower the only defences were the Iron Age ditch and bank.

4

The Great Siege of 1216

When William the Conqueror had reached Dover in the autumn of 1066, the defenders had speedily surrendered. One hundred and fifty years later, when another invading army from across the Channel captured the town, both the castle and its garrison were made of sterner stuff. The events of 1216–17 were to ensure enduring fame for Hubert de Burgh the Constable and were to lead to the last great medieval strengthening of the castle's defences.

In the autumn of 1215, after the Barons had largely disavowed Magna Carta and with civil war looming, King John had hurried to south east Kent to secure local support and to gather his continental mercenaries. September he spent at Canterbury and Dover seeing to their defences. At Dover he must have found the new outer walls largely complete, but it is likely that work yet remained to be done on the new north gate barbican. John probably augmented the garrison before leaving at the end of the month after learning of the seizure of Rochester by the rebels.

The king's campaign began with the spectacularly successful siege and capture of Rochester Castle. The Barnwell chronicler noted in some awe, 'Our age has not known a siege so hard pressed nor so strongly resisted.' After it, he added, 'Few cared to put their trust in castles'. Few castles indeed cared to resist the king and, by the spring of 1216, the rebels were left only with London. But on 21 May, Prince Louis and his French army landed at Thanet to join the rebels. John, watching events from the Kent coast, returned to Dover briefly before withdrawing to Winchester.

At Dover Castle, the king left a substantial garrison – accounts mention 140 knights and a large number of men-at-arms. The castle was well stocked with food and munitions, and as evidence of its importance, King John left command of the garrison in the hands of Hubert de Burgh, Justiciar of England. Nevertheless, it was not an encouraging prospect: by late summer, with French aid, the rebels had recaptured their territory and in south-east England, only Windsor and Dover held out.

At Dover, Louis himself initially directed the siege. Establishing his headquarters in Dover Priory, he split his forces. Some remained in the town, but the rest set up camp, probably on the high ground to the north east of the castle out of arrow range from the garrison.

With the French fleet offshore and a French army encircling them, the garrison had little hope of fresh supplies or reinforcements. This however, did not appear to dampen their offensive spirit. A contemporary chronicler, probably a Flemish soldier in John's service, recorded the garrison making frequent sorties from the north gateway barbican. Although moated, this barbican only had a timber palisade and had clearly been constructed in haste as war loomed.

The castle's major weakness lay in its position below the crest of the hill (see **5**); Louis sought to exploit this and concentrated his attack on the north gateway. Judging by the extent of rebuilding here by Henry III, the north-east curtain as far as the later Fitzwilliam Gateway must also have been extensively damaged.

The French mangonels, perriers and trebuchets were probably positioned a little to the north-east of the castle, perhaps where the modern barracks stand. While these weapons were being assembled, other craftsmen were busy constructing a great movable tower or belfry, protected by hurdles and with a covered gallery or drawbridge to enable assault troops to pour onto the top of the curtain wall. While the attention of the garrison was on these elaborate and public preparations, Louis had his company of miners burrow into the chalk and undermine the palisades of the barbican.

These careful preparations by the French were duly rewarded. The timber palisade, even without being undermined, would not have long resisted missiles lobbed by the siege engines. With the barbican defences splintered and crumbling, a direct assault by Louis' knights led to its capture. The garrison licked its wounds and withdrew behind the main stone walls

Prolonged sieges have always attracted spectators; Dover was no exception. As the weeks passed, the garrison looking out from the top of the keep would have seen a steady stream of nobles from both sides of the Channel being shown round the siege works and the tented camp. More dispiriting was the arrival of the king of Scotland, Alexander II, to do homage to the French claimant.

After the storming of the barbican there was probably a lull for a few days as engineers repositioned the siege engines to concentrate their fire on the north gateway itself. But however effective the relentless battering of this heavy artillery, it was the French miners who again played a crucial role. Tunnelling into the soft chalk, they undermined the eastern gate tower.

It would seem that the garrison was well aware of their intentions, for small tunnels from within the castle, which still survive today, are best interpreted as countermines dug in the hope of breaking into the French tunnel. In this, they were apparently unsuccessful. The mine was sprung and the gatetower collapsed into the ditch. As it did, Louis' forces poured over the damaged barbican and through the new breech. This was the critical moment for the garrison, one for which Hubert de Burgh must have been preparing.

In what was clearly bitter hand-to-hand fighting, the garrison fought back, combat ebbing and flowing in the comparatively confined space between the north gateway and the inner barbican to King's Gate. Perhaps unable to channel sufficent reinforcements through the breech – there is no record of the belfry being used, which would imply the infilling of part of the ditch – perhaps surprised by the ferocity of the garrison's resistance, Louis' forces were put to flight. In the words of the chronicler, 'the people inside drove them out with great vigour, and then closed up the place where their walls had fallen, with great timbers, and crossbeams, and palisades of oak trunks'.

This was to prove the climax of the siege, although it was far from over. Afterwards, both sides buried their dead – a number of French knights being taken back to France for burial – and the garrison strengthened the damaged perimeter. For Louis, the siege was becoming increasingly unsatisfactory. The garrison clearly had no intention of surrendering, while Louis's own supply lines to the west were being increasingly harried by irregular forces under the command of the near-mythical William of Kensham, Willikin of the Weald.

Probably early in September 1216 a truce was arranged to allow the garrison to seek fresh orders from King John. But on 16 October, John died at Newark Castle and his son Henry III was proclaimed king. At Dover, the truce was extended and in November Hubert de Burgh was at last able to leave the castle he had commanded so valiantly to travel to

Bristol to take up his role as Justiciar to the nine-year-old king.

In April 1217, as skirmishing resumed, Louis returned from France with his father. As his fleet passed Dover, where the local truce still held, he was just in time to see guerilla forces from the Weald set his camp ablaze. Landing at Sandwich, Louis again extended the truce, but it must have been obvious to him that the castle would have to be stormed if only to stop further attempts at relieving the garrison. On 12 May he returned to Dover to resume operations. But three days later, defeat of French forces at the battle of Lincoln signalled the end of the war. As soon as news reached Dover, Louis raised the siege and left for London. Dover castle, after a year of sieges and truces, remained untaken if not unscarred.

5

The completed medieval fortress

The siege of 1216–17 had demonstrated, all too clearly, the vulnerability of Dover's northern defences. Under less resolute defenders the castle would surely have fallen. The shock of this spurred Henry III to a further major programme of modifications and additions which from 1217 to early 1221 were personally supervised by Hubert de Burgh. To finance construction, the Kent scutage, or payment in lieu of military service, was diverted to the castle. So, too, were the entire revenues of Norfolk, Suffolk and Kent – all counties where Hubert was sheriff. Part of the substantial sums raised by these means went on the garrison, its equipment and stores, but it seems that between 1217 and 1221 around £1365 was spent on the fabric. Work was to go on continuously for nearly 40 years, and over £6000 was to be poured into Dover. Well before then, it must have been hoped that 'the key of England' as it was so aptly described by the contemporary chronicler Matthew Paris, would never again be capable of being turned by an attacker.

First and most important, the northern gateway had to be secured and an alternative entrance provided which was not so vulnerable to attack from the high ground. Then the outer walls had to be extended south to the cliff edge and finally defences round the church and *pharos* had to be made far stronger to prevent them becoming a stronghold for an enemy who had penetrated the outer fortifications.

Building accounts indicate that work began first on the new gatehouse, for until it was in operation the North Gateway could not be sealed. By 1220, stone for the new entrance and its barbican was being shipped from Folkestone, and by 1227 they were complete (**19**).

Hubert chose the location for the new gateway with considerable skill, placing it on the western side of the castle, where it was well sheltered from the high ground to the north east. Outside, the steep scarp falling away from it made direct attack that much more difficult. Even so, no chances were taken with its design and Constable's Gateway emerged as one of the strongest in the country.

The heart of Constable's Gateway is one of King John's mural towers through which Hubert's engineers cut the new gate passage. Extra protection was given by two attached D-shaped towers set forward of this, facing north and south along the deepened ditch, their backs joined over the roadway, the foundations for their spurred bases set deep in the chalk in the bottom of the ditch. North and south of this trinity of towers, three further semicircular towers with spurred bases were built linking into the reformed curtain and set back from the main gateway. On the more vulnerable northern side, the engineers placed two of the towers, one of which was considerably larger than the other. Like the new outer gate towers, all were well equipped with arrow slits.

A hall and chambers for the Constable and

19 *Constable's Gateway, built to replace the North Gateway after the siege of 1216–17. It was extensively modernised in 1883–4.*

his household were built into the rear of this massive complex. Also provided were guard-rooms, a portcullis chamber and space for working the draw-bridge which rested on the still-surviving medieval pier set in the centre of the ditch (**20**). Outside lay an elaborate barbican; this was to be extensively reformed at the end of the eighteenth century.

Constable's Gateway marked a significant advance in castle defence. As with the earlier Avranches Tower, the proliferation of arrow slits gave the defenders enormous fire-power, while the outer pair of towers, set forward in the moat, enabled enfilading fire to rake the ditch. Compared to the north gateway of 20

years earlier, it vastly increased the garrison's ability to resist attack. Its design clearly owed much to lessons learnt in the siege and was to be copied twenty years later in construction of the Black Gate at Newcastle. Although Constable's Gateway was to have its accommodation remodelled in the 1880s, its towers largely escaped reduction in the eighteenth century, and it best preserves the formidable appearance which the whole of medieval Dover Castle must have retained until then.

No doubt as soon as the new entrance was ready, military engineers began to secure the northern gateway. This time, they took no chances. The ruined eastern tower was rebuilt in solid masonry, while the gateway itself was blocked by a solid beaked tower firmly keyed in to its two neighbours. For long, this trinity of towers continued to be known as 'the old gateway'; more recently they have been known as the Norfolk Towers. Beyond them, an elaborate detached earthwork was formed to give defenders better control of the high ground to the north and to prevent easy access to the northern tip of the castle by miners and heavy artillery.

Although the accounts are unclear, it seems probable that while the work on the gateways was in progress, other masons, labourers and fossatores had begun reprofiling the main ditches and extending the outer curtain walls steadily southwards to the cliff edge. These curtain walls were to be lowered by Georgian military engineers over 500 years later, but the differing designs of the surviving mural towers suggests a long construction period and several different military engineers.

In the late 1220s, between 200 and 300 *fossatores* – diggers and labourers – were at work under the direction of Ralf of Popeshal. This number suggests a likely date for the great earthwork being thrown round the southern side of the *pharos* and church, sweeping away

20 *The ground plan of Constable's Gateway.*

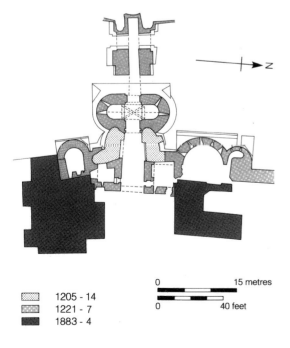

▓	1205 - 14
▒	1221 - 7
■	1883 - 4

0   15 metres

0   40 feet

whatever remained of the eleventh-century defences here. Although not mentioned in documentary accounts (see **colour plate 1**) the bank is securely dated on archaeological grounds to the first half of the thirteenth century. It was certainly in existence in 1256 when its timber palisade was replaced by a stone wall, the footings of which can still be seen. These defences were linked on the western side by a wall which ran to Colton's Gate before turning north to Harcourt Tower where it joined the defences running west to Peverell's Tower and the main outer curtain. On the eastern side, there was a similar arrangement. A wall linked Clinton's Tower, which lay north east of the church, with Ashford Tower on the main eastern curtain. Although the last two towers along with Harcourt Tower have long been demolished, as has most of the curtain wall save in the immediate vicinity of Colton's Gateway, the earthworks still remain. Completion here enabled the southern half of the castle to be isolated if necessary and provided a triple line of defences south of the keep.

These post-siege works, spread over nearly forty years, transformed the castle and marked the high-water mark of its medieval fortifications. They gave it the appearance it still largely retains today, despite alterations by later Georgian and Victorian military engineers (**21**).

Only some of Henry III's officials are known to us by name. The direction of the works was entrusted to the resident constables, but they were aided by men such as Richard of Narford – presumably a Norfolk man – and Jocelyn de Oye. These, described as keepers of the works, combined the modern roles of military engineers, architects and quantity surveyors. They changed the castle's defensive capabilities while revolutionising its offensive powers.

The systematic use of mural towers, begun here under Henry II, allowed defenders to cover the intervening lengths of curtain wall

21 *The castle from the north showing the great thirteenth-century bank around the church and* pharos. *This 1988 photograph, taken after extensive scrub clearance, demonstrates the tremendous scale of the outlying eighteenth- and nineteenth-century earthworks.*

with their weapons, and thus prevent a besieger getting too close. Deep ditches were similarly dug to keep attackers from the walls and, more importantly, as a deterrent against mining. The 1216 siege though demonstrated two glaring weaknesses: first, the chalk subsoil was all too easily mined. Second, the one main gateway allowed the besiegers to concentrate troops outside it, thus preventing the garrison from wresting any initiative by sallying forth in strength.

In the reconstruction, extra gateways were provided for such sorties. To have any hope of success, these sally ports had to be dispersed to stretch the besiegers' forces and they had to be so designed that the garrison could assemble unseen and retain the vital element of surprise. On the western side, to the rear of Constable's Tower engineers constructed a tunnel leading down beneath the gateway to an exit below the drawbridge. This not only enabled fire to be directed upwards at attackers approaching the bridge, but also allowed the garrison to sortie into the western ditch.

On the opposite side of the castle, engineers inserted a second gateway flanked by two keel-shaped towers and with living accommodation over the passageway. Although long known as Fitzwilliam Gate, after a late fifteenth-century Deputy-Constable, Philip Fitzwilliam, it was clearly designed to have a double role as a postern. The bridge connecting it with the outer bank of the ditch was originally covered so that troops crossing could remain unseen and protected. Traces of the vaulted roof still remain (**colour plate 5**). From its lower gateway, set deep in the outer bank, the garrison could sally forth to attack any besiegers at the northen end of the castle.

The most elaborate arrangements were, not surprisingly, found at the old north entrance. North of the ditch, the engineers formed a substantial defensible spur or outwork. In the centre of the ditch they built a circular tower, St John's Tower, its parapets sufficently high to enable archers to overlook the spur and with sallyports giving access to the ditch. From the castle a tunnel led under the old north gateway, emerging through the bank into a short roofed passage into the south side of St John's Tower. From there a drawbridge connected with a bridge to a tunnel into the Spur. Gates in the tunnels provided further protection. Traces of these features still remain despite alterations in the eighteenth century.

Within the Spur the medieval tunnel divided into three passages which fanned out to the north, suggesting three separate exits, one possibly linked with a long-vanished tower shown in early prints.

Within the castle the present spiral staircase to these northern tunnels is entirely nineteenth-century. The original access arrangements are unknown. It is tempting to suggest that the stone bridge from King's Gate barbican which now stops abruptly behind the Norfolk Towers, might have given access to earlier steps to the tunnels (see **4**). If this was covered, like the Fitzwilliam Gate bridge, it would have given the garrison unseen access to the spur

from within the inner ward, possibly safeguarding these communications even if the outer ward had fallen into enemy hands.

Such elaborate tunnels cannot be paralleled in any other English medieval fortification; completion gave the garrison the flexibility for sorties that had been lacking in 1216. The chalk subsoil made the tunnels possible, but it was the importance of the castle and the shock of the siege which had spurred their construction (see **28**).

Documents refer to the construction of other vanished parts of the defences, but also to the modernisation and extension of accommodation within the castle. In 1221 the castle oven was repaired; six years later comes construction of a new granary 'in order to keep the corn in the castle sweeter', and in 1234 a windmill is built for grinding it.

The largest expenditure was on a new hall and chamber for the king on the eastern side of the inner bailey; these were completed in 1240. The king's private chamber backed onto the curtain wall north-east of the keep and largely replaced a building constructed here early in the thirteenth century for King John. The private chamber was probably linked by a pentice or passage to a private chapel and to the Great Hall built against the curtain to the south. Thirteenth-century documents refer to two chapels in the castle, one dedicated to St Thomas, the other to St Andrew; these could be the two chapels within the forebuilding, but it is more likely that the chapel of St Andrew is the long-vanished private chapel connected to the king's private chamber.

From the fourteenth century onwards the Great Hall was known as Arthur's Hall; it was a substantial structure measuring internally some 77ft by 30ft (23m by 9m), by 1365 roofed in shingles (see **13**). Parts of this building, notably the screen wall at the southern end with its three doorways leading through to buttery, kitchen and pantry, were later to be preserved below the eighteenth-century barracks where they can still be seen.

Construction of the new hall reflected Henry III's desire for more spacious and well-lit quarters than those in the keep (**colour plate 6**). Above the Great Hall porch there was a private oratory. The sixteenth-century Bereblock print clearly shows this building with a pentice leading to the keep. In 1244, construction of a new kitchen in the south eastern corner of the inner bailey marked completion of these modernisation works. Probably contemporary with it are the underground cisterns beneath the adjacent barracks. These doubtless provided water for the kitchen, and were probably replenished by rainwater from the roofs.

Immediately west of Palace Gate, the eighteenth-century barracks incorporate a substantial amount of medieval work. In the eastern gable wall is a blocked thirteenth-century window and a heavily modernised doorway of similar date. It is tempting to identify this as 'Arthur's Lesser Hall'.

The building accounts for all these works, although incomplete, give us fascinating glimpses into a vast construction project spread over many years. Bills for sand and lime, the carriage of stone by sea to Dover and its subsequent transport up Castle Hill, along with tubs of water, lead and nails, timbers and flints, all have frequent entries. Alongside these feature masons and carpenters, lime-burners and thatchers, ditch-diggers and labourers, smiths and plumbers, carters and watchmen, hod and barrow men. Other entries refer to work on specific parts of the castle and to the re-use of materials: 'for an old ship bought in the town of Dover to plank the said tower, 42s ... For guarding that ship on the shore for eight nights before it could be broken up, 14d.' Important members of the garrison were provided with housing: 'And to two carpenters ... for making the house of Gerard the Crossbowman ...' More romantic is an entry for 23 June 1221: 'And for buying the house of Bartholomew the Janitor which was his wife's, when they went to Jerusalem, 6s.8d.'

For all this expenditure, Henry III must have felt justifiable satisfaction. The castle's defences made it one of the most formidable fortifications in western Europe, while its position high on the cliffs made it a prominent landmark to seafarers in the Straits, a vivid symbol of English royal power (**colour plate 7**).

6

Life in medieval Dover Castle

For all its elaborate defences, the strength of Dover Castle depended ultimately on the size and morale of the garrison, the quality of leadership and the amount of stores and equipment available. Leadership and morale vary according to personalities and the task in hand, while stores and equipment depend on an efficient commissariat.

In the fourteenth century, when the defences remained much as completed by Henry III, it was calculated that the outer bailey required 832 men to man the battlements, allowing a ratio of three men to every two battlements. The inner bailey and keep were said to have a further 378 battlements, giving a total of 1394 soldiers in the unlikely event of all battlements needing to be fully manned simultaneously. In practice, it is unlikely in the medieval period that garrison numbers ever approached that figure. In the siege of 1216-17, admittedly with a smaller fortification to defend, 140 knights and what was described as 'a great number of men-at-arms' just sufficed to hold Dover. Louis' forces were probably faced at most by no more than 500 men within the castle.

As a royal fortress, responsibility for garrisoning Dover Castle rested with the monarch. In practice, this was a task which fell to the constable or his deputy. In wartime, the king might provide troops, either from whatever army he had raised at the time, or from among the retainers of his supporters. Failing all else, the royal exchequer would hire mercenaries, as

happened in 1216.

Maintaining a peacetime garrison presented different problems. No medieval English monarch kept a standing army, save for the knights and men-at-arms in his immediate entourage. Yet a strategic castle such as Dover needed the nucleus of a permanent garrison to represent the king's authority and doubtless to keep an eye on travellers landing at Dover. The peripatetic nature of medieval royal courts too, meant that Dover castle was frequently visited by the monarch. The thirteenth-century Statutes of the castle indicate that sometimes there was little warning of such royal descents:

> If the king arrives unexpectedly in the night, the great gates shall not be opened to him, but he shall go to the postern called the King's Gate [now Fitzwilliam Gate], towards the north and there the Constable and those who accompany him, may admit the king and a certain number of his suite. When the king is admitted he has the command, and in the morning, when it is full day, he may admit the remainder of his company.

For the two centuries or so after the Conquest of 1066, royal and baronial castles relied for their core garrisons on castle-guard. This feudal service, owed by larger estates, entailed the provision of knights and their men-at-arms to man particular castles, normally for forty days each year. It was rarely popular as it was time-consuming and could involve considerable travel from home – part of the castle-guard at Dover was owed by knights from Northamptonshire. Its efficency, too, may be doubted if there was not a resident Constable able to weld the disparate and ever-changing groups under his command into an effective force familiar with the castle.

It was not until the civil wars of Stephen and Mathilda (1135–54), that the king appointed the first of the resident Constables of Dover castle. These men rarely had estates sufficent to provide castle-guard and initially, they seem to have been supported by Exchequer grants to defray garrison costs. Henry II sought to rationalise these arrangements for he had at his disposal two great estates, one formerly belonging to the Montforts, the other to Bishop Odo. Fifty-six knights' fees from the former, known as the 'Honor Constabularie' initially were allocated to general defence of the country, but by the begining of the thirteenth century were apparently devoted to Dover alone.

In 1166, Henry II allocated lands of Bishop Odo specifically to Dover. These arrangements produced a further 118 knights' fees, so that in theory over 170 knights and probably roughly the same number of soldiers could be produced. Spread evenly across the year, this suggests a peacetime garrison of around 14 knights forming the nucleus of a larger number of foot-soldiers, warders and porters.

Records show the majority of the knights' fees were from lands in Kent; the names of some of the baronies on which these were centred live on in the names of the castle towers – Avranches, Fulbert, Peverell, Mamignot, Crevecoeur and Fitzwilliam, a roll-call of the upper end of the Angevin aristocracy.

For over half-a-century castle-guard remained the back-bone of the Dover garrison. But after the 1216 siege, Hubert de Burgh sought further reform. A charter of that year made plain the defects of the existing system and proposed a solution:

And [Hubert] considering it was not safe for the Castle at different months to have new guards to ward, procured with the consent of the King ... that every Knight due for ward of one month should pay ten shillings, and that henceforth certain men chosen and sworn, both Knights and foot soldiers, should be hired for guarding the Castle.

This marked the start of a professional standing garrison for Dover, financed by the money payment called Castleward rent. This system remained throughout the Middle Ages, only falling into disuse in the late fifteenth century as the military importance of the castle itself declined.

The Statutes of Dover Castle, attributed to Stephen de Pencestre, Constable from 1265 to 1298, provide a fascinating picture of garrison life. Of the 22 statutes or rules for daily life, no less than 14 are concerned with the church of St Mary-in-Castro and its priests:

XIX The priests are to pray for the recovery of the Holy Land, the success of Christianity, the king and Royal family, the Barons of the Realm, the Constable and all the Garrison.

Other statutes detail the conduct expected of members of the garrison:

VI Either sergeant or warder using vile language shall be brought before the Constable, who shall have the matter considered ... He who was in the wrong shall lose his day's pay – if the Constable so wills

But the kernel of the rules lies in the first few statutes which tell us how the castle was to be guarded:

I At sunset the bridge shall be drawn, and the gates shut; afterwards the guard shall be mounted by twenty warders on the castle walls.

II Any warder found outside the walls, or otherwise off his guard, shall be put in the Donjon prison, and punished besides in body and goods at the Constable's discretion …

III After the last mount, two sergeants shall turn out of their houses to serve as chief guards. They shall make continual rounds within the Castle to visit the warders on the walls and see that they right loyally keep their watch without going to sleep …

IV It is established by ancient rule that if a chief guard discover a warder asleep, he shall take something from him as he lies … or cut a piece out of part of his clothes, to witness against him in case the warder should deny having been asleep, and he shall lose his day's wage, viz 2d.

V And if it happen that the sergeant will not make such arrest, for pity's sake, … then he shall be brought before the Constable, and be sentenced to prison 'dur et fort', after which he shall be led to the Great Gate (Constable's Gate), in the presence of the garrison, and there be expelled from the Castle …

These rules make clear the concern about surprise attacks by night. In the eighteenth century, sentry boxes were provided on the walls. There is no record of such conveniences in the thirteenth century, and for most of the year the warders on the walls must have had a fairly miserable time, given their exposed position.

In daytime, there was less need for so many sentries, and in peacetime the porters at Constable's Gate were the ears and eyes of the castle. Their duties were clearly defined in another contemporary document:

The porters at the gate shall not suffer any persons to enter, until they have taken particular notice of them, and if they be strangers they shall not step within the sill of the wicket, but one of the Porters is to call the Constable, and in his absence, his lieutenant; but every person seeking admittance is to receive civil treatment … The gates are never to be left during the day to the care of any persons but the porters, and they are always to have the wicket secured with bolts. After the bridge is drawn up and the great gates shut, they are not to be opened until the rising of the sun.

Stephen de Pencestre had good reason for refining the garrison duties, for his role as Constable was now combined with Wardenship of the Cinque Ports. That loose association of the original five ports had grown steadily in power, independence and arrogance to central government. Keeping the Channel safe was frequently an excuse for general piracy, something which no strong monarch could tolerate for long. At first, the Cinque Ports regulated their affairs with a Warden chosen by themselves. But the dangers of such an arrangement became all too obvious during the baronial uprisings at the end of Henry III's reign in the 1260s. Then, both sides sought to control the Cinque Ports, main entry routes for foreign mercenaries, while the barons also wished to have the appointment of the Constable of Dover. In 1261 Henry III was forced to march on the castle and replace the baronial candidate with Sir Robert Walerand. As soon as order was restored, the king ended this damaging duality of power on the Kent coast by making one man responsible for both castle and ports. From the time of Stephen de Pencestre onwards, the offices were never again separate and their gift remained firmly in the king's hands.

By the late thirteenth century, the Constable's job was complex and demanding. Although his primary responsibility lay in looking after the castle, his duties extended much further. He oversaw traffic in the Channel and was responsible for the defence of the coastline of south east England. Frequently, he was sheriff of Kent or Sussex. His post as Warden of the Cinque Ports extended to Hastings in one direction, and round to the coast of Essex in the other. He was President of the Court of Shepway, the principal administrative tool of the Cinque Port federation.

Dover Castle itself lay outside both the jurisdiction of the county and the Cinque Ports; its priests, too, were under lay jurisdiction. To deal with discipline, a 'Court of the Castle Gate' was established, probably by Stephen de Pencestre. By the fourteenth century it met once a fortnight and dealt with much of the Cinque Ports business, mostly cases of debts and trespass.

To share the burdens of office, a lieutenant or deputy Constable played an increasingly important role, taking over tasks such as ensuring the castle remained in good repair. For this, the thirteenth century statutes are quite explicit:

> The Lieutenant-Governor, the Clerk of the Exchequer, the Marshall, the Carpenter, and other artificers, are, at times appointed (once a week), to survey the walls of the Castle, both within and without, and shall order the necessary repairs of all houses and buildings.

In the early eighteenth century, when the Lords' Warden's role had become largely ceremonial, the Lord Warden took over Walmer Castle as a more comfortable residence, while retaining the title of Constable of Dover. The deputy-Constable remained at Dover, ocupying the quarters above Constable's Gate where his successors continue to reside.

At the height of its medieval importance, Dover Castle housed an extensive community within its walls. Both the Constable and the deputy-Constable had their own households which were the focus for a far larger resident population. This included priests for the castle chapels and St Mary-in-Castro, as well as the porters and warders. The latter, part of the permanent guard, formed the most conspicuous element. To these can probably be added 'the Carpenter and other artificers' mentioned in the thirteenth century statutes. 'Other artificers' may well have included stone masons,

plumbers and labourers, although many of these probably lived in the town.

Many of the mural towers had fireplaces and garderobes, showing that they were always intended to have a residential role. Accounts mention 'repairing houses about the castle', while there are other specific references to particular structures: the castle oven, a brewhouse, a turf-house, a well-house – which needed 500 sheaves of straw for its thatch in 1283 – a granary and a barn. A more mysterious entry was payment for '61 beams for the hermit's house', while a reference to the castle lawn provides a glimpse of a softer side to life here. An entry in 1365 refers to thatching houses adjacent to the church, a reminder that the immediate surroundings of St Mary-in-Castro were once very different from the existing open spaces.

As the administrative hub of the area, the castle saw a steady flow of people: messengers from the king, officials from the Cinque Ports, traders and merchants, petitioners and those attending the court. Dover was also host to the monarch and his senior officials. Sometimes, the royal visit was part of a royal progress, at other times it was specifically to welcome distinguished visitors entering the country. More often, it was a convenient hotel for court officials and embassies waiting favourable weather to cross to the Continent. Long after it had declined in military importance, buildings in the castle were kept in repair and occasionally modernised largely so that it could retain this role as a staging post.

Although the reforming of the castle's defences was largely completed by the 1250s, there continued to be fairly heavy expenditure for most of the rest of the thirteenth century. Large quantities of timber was sent from royal forests in Essex, probably mostly to repair floors and roofs affected by rot, a constant problem in the castle to this day. In 1294 a stone tower-mill was built just south of the church; this apparently survived until demolished by the Board of Ordnance in the 1770s.

In the fourteenth and fifteenth centuries, defence efforts here centred on fortifying the town with a wall and gateways (see **71**). The first indication that work was under way was in 1324; further references to construction and repair continue to 1483, but the town walls seem to have had a surprisingly short life. The antiquary Leland, writing in the mid sixteenth century, was uncertain of their extent. However, construction of the dual carriageway along Townwall Street in 1992 revealed substantial sections below ground still remaining to a height of 19ft (6m).

Not surprisingly, the cost of maintenance of the castle was an ever-present factor. Despite its continuous occupation, the surviving documents for its later medieval history record periods of disrepair. These tended to be followed by formal inquiries which recommended that large sums be spent; these in turn usually led to the provision of lesser sums and a blitz on the worst of the fabric by the king's craftsmen or by workmen impressed locally by the constable. Much of the documented repairs relate to vanished buildings or are untraceable on the monument. Most was the normal maintenance to be expected on a fortress singularly exposed to the elements, but in May 1382 what was clearly a quite severe earthquake shook the castle. Nicholas Payntour, the master mason, and his staff spent 44 days repairing damaged walls and battlements.

Stephen de Pencestre was quite exceptional in being Constable for 33 years (1265–98); the medieval average was less than four, with some constables in office for under two years, and others largely absentees. Stephen's long tenure probably saw the castle better maintained and its garrison better organised than at any other period. He was closely involved with the Cinque Ports and was instrumental in founding New Winchelsea in the 1290s.

In the fifteenth century Humphrey, Duke of Gloucester, was Constable for 22 years (1415–37). Surviving accounts suggest he was diligent in looking after the castle. Among his interests was the maintenance of a large clock which helped regulate the hours of the garrison. His surviving memorial is the rebuilt top of the Roman *pharos* where he added the existing octagonal upper storey with its five windows (see **3**). This work was undertaken between 1426 and 1437 to provide a new belfry for the adjacent church.

Later in the fifteenth century, although very largely undocumented, the main apartments of the castle underwent a further modernisation, almost certainly at the request of the king. In the keep are a number of late fifteenth-century windows and doorways, while three of the four massive fireplaces on the first and second floors have carved in their spandrels Edward IV's Yorkist badge of the rose en soleil. Edward IV, his troubled reign punctuated by exile in the Netherlands, had better cause than many to appreciate the strategic importance of his great Kentish fortress, although he also spent lavishly at Fotheringhay and Nottingham as well as at Windsor and Eltham. The modernisation of Dover keep's accommodation, with improved lighting and heating, would have brought it up to the standards then expected by the king and his court.

A hundred years later, William Darell, chaplain to Elizabeth I, wrote that Edward IV had spent over £10,000 on the castle. Some of this was on repairs, although Darell says that the king entirely rebuilt Clopton's Tower. This, now Treasurer's Tower, shows signs of extensive late medieval repair. Near Palace Gate he also 'erected a stately tower, furnished with handsome apartments, and adorned it with the figures of lions and fleurs-de-lys'. There is no reason to disbelieve Darell who probably had first-hand knowledge of the castle.

Just over ten years after Edward IV's death in 1483, the French army under Charles VII invaded northern Italy accompanied for the first time by a powerful siege train of heavy artillery. The effect was instantaneous: existing fortifications crumbled; sieges were over in days. It was clear to everyone that fortifications

had to be radically redesigned, not just to withstand the effect of sustained gunfire but also to be able to mount the new weapons effectively. Existing defences largely became obsolete and Dover was no exception (**22**).

22 *Dover's most famous gun: 'Queen Elizabeth's Pocket Pistol'. This 12pdr brass Basilisk was cast at Utrecht in 1544 and first appeared at the castle in 1612. For conservation reasons it is now displayed under cover.*

7

The castle in the doldrums 1500–1740

By 1500, most of the defences of Dover Castle were between 250 and 300 years old. In large measure, they and the accommodation within had been kept in reasonable repair. But the battle of Bosworth in 1485 did not just herald a change of dynasty: it coincided with a revolution in weapons and fortifications, the implications of which were not lost on the first two Tudor monarchs.

Both Henry VII and Henry VIII were keenly interested in ordnance – in 1496 Henry VII ordered Henry Fyner, Goldsmith of Southwark, to set up a blast furnace on the Ashdown Forest at Newbridge in Sussex to cast iron shot and fittings for gun carriages for the king's new artillery train. Within a few years, the Weald was producing cast-iron guns for the Crown. Mangonels, trebuchets and most of the paraphernalia of medieval siegecraft rapidly passed into history. The hand-guns and small artillery pieces, in limited use in castles and town defences since the late fourteenth century, were no match for the new and vastly more powerful weapons. Most existing fortifications had neither the space to mount them nor, more importantly, the strength to resist artillery bombardment.

Henry VII was also the first English monarch to create a permanent Royal Navy, a policy enthusiastically endorsed by his son. In part, this was a deliberate extension of direct royal control, in part it was a realisation that ship design was changing. In the middle of the fifteenth century, when guns first began to be used at sea, they were small anti-personnel weapons, often fixed on swivels. By 1500, larger weapons were being mounted broadside to fire through embrasures in the gunwales. In 1511, the *Mary Rose* and the *Peter Pomegranate* were completed, the first ships to be built with two tiers of broadside armament, the lower tier firing through gunports in the sides of the ships. This revolutionary development marked the effective end of the medieval ship which had been able to do double duty as a merchant ship, and then be called up as a fighting ship in the king's service in time of war. From now on, warships were of specialised design: merchant ships could no longer form the nucleus of the royal battle fleet, although they played an important auxiliary role until the end of the sixteenth century. The increasingly specialised requirements of warships led Henry VII to establish a royal dockyard at Portsmouth in 1495. This was followed by further yards at Woolwich in 1513, Deptford in 1517 and Chatham in 1547. With the establishment of a permanent royal navy and means of building and maintaining it, the importance of the Cinque Ports as providers of ships to defend the Channel was at an end.

All these new factors also reduced dramatically the value of Dover as a fortress. That it survived at all when the majority of other royal castles fell into decay is a reflection both of its strategic location and the convenience of its accommodation. The post of Constable became seen increasingly as an honorarium, a reward for services to the king, rather than as an important military position; practical duties at Dover effectively were delegated to the Lieutenant or deputy-Constable.

In the turmoils of the 1530s, high office in Henry's government could be risky, and the Constableship was no exception. In 1534, George Boleyn, Lord Rochford, brother of Anne Boleyn, was plucked from comparative obscurity and made Warden and Constable. Dover was convenient for his official journeys to France on Henry's behalf, but George's fate was inextricably linked with the fortunes of his sister. In May 1536, he was arrested, accused of incest with Anne and, along with four other alleged paramours was executed two days before the queen. As William Darell lugubriously noted, 'scarce had he spread his sails to the soft inviting gales of fortune, when the dark clouds of adversity began to gather round him; for in a short time he was not only stripped of the honours and offices that had been conferred upon him, but brought to the block and beheaded.'

Despite finance for defence being focused elsewhere, accounts for the castle show that money continued to be spent on maintenance. In 1536 there were apparently some 460 workmen here when there was a request for two old 'hales' or tents for the men to work in during bad weather, and to provide covered dining areas to save the men going into the town for their meal which took up much time.

Considerable sums tended to be spent before royal visits: between 1532 and 1544 Henry VIII came to Dover on eight occasions. In December 1539 an iron crown was erected over the King's Lodgings in the keep before the arrival of Anne of Cleves. Documentary accounts suggest that the royal apartments were rearranged according to the latest fashion, divided into two sets, each with chamber, privy chamber and bedchamber for Henry VIII and his current queen.

Much of the summer of 1539 was spent repairing the outer walls and towers. Underpinning, pointing and galletting – inserting flint chippings into the wider mortar joints – were undertaken, while Colton's Gateway was overhauled. Although this work was connected with the invasion scare that year, the main thrust of Henry's defence proposals was elsewhere. His new artillery fortresses at Sandown, Deal and Walmer commanded the sheltered waters within the Goodwin Sands, while to the west of Folkestone, Sandgate Castle was carefully sited to overlook the coastal road where it left the low levels of the Romney Marsh and climbed over the hills to Dover. Dover Harbour, then in the course of construction and one of the most remarkable feats of Tudor engineering, was protected by three bulwarks or gun batteries at harbour level. The surviving but altered Moat's Bulwark together with Archcliffe Fort date from this 1539–40 campaign. The whole emphasis of the defence scheme was for artillery to engage enemy ships, or failing that, to fire at enemy troops as soon as they had landed. The old castle on its cliff-top site was largely ignored, although the 'Tudor Bulwark' or gun-platform which juts into the west moat near the cliff edge may date from this time. The castle's accommodation however was used by the king's officials supervising the new defences.

Only late in Henry's reign were a number of guns mounted in the castle. A 1548 report mentions a total of nine weapons, apparently mounted near the cliff-edge to give a plunging fire into the bay; the bulwark could perhaps have accommodated two or three of these.

Well into the seventeenth century, most of the medieval buildings, especially in Keep Yard, continued in use. Elizabeth I visited the castle in 1573, staying as a guest of Lord Cobham. Significantly, in 1582 when she returned to say farewell to the Duke of Alençon, she stayed in the town. This visit coincided with another burst of repair activity: St Mary-in-Castro, then known as King Lucius' Church, had extensive repairs, as did many of the towers at the northern end of the castle. The *pharos* was roofed, floored and rendered externally to convert it to a gunpowder magazine, while the exterior of the keep ('Caesar's Tower' to the Elizabethans) also had its external render repaired. Expenditure continued at intervals to the end of Elizabeth's reign, well justifying the Kentish historian William Lambarde's observation in 1596 that 'our gracious Queene Elizabeth hath beene at great charge in repairing the castle.'

In 1624, George Villiers, Duke of Buckingham, was appointed Constable. Then at the height of his power and influence, he was to be the last Constable to lavish money on the castle's accommodation. Between December 1624 and October 1625 considerable sums were spent, some probably on the lodgings in Constable's Tower. There is also record of bricklayers and earthworkers; but there are no further details. Although such people may suggest the construction of earthwork fortifications, it could be that the earthworkers were simply recutting and clearing existing ditches.

However, the main work was the modernisation of the keep in preparation for Henrietta Maria of France. In December 1624 she was formally betrothed to Prince Charles and it was clear that she would need to be accommodated at the castle on her arrival in England. The substantial sum of £2600 was allocated to ensure that it was suitable for this important occasion. It seems likely that Inigo Jones, then Surveyor of the King's Works, may have been involved; certainly control of the work was retained in Whitehall rather than being left to the Constable.

Time was short, with the builders having a little over six months to attempt to modernise the accommodation. They began with the forebuilding as this would be the first part of the keep to be seen by the French royal party. At the entrance they constructed a 'greate Rusticke Dore' some 23ft (7m) high and 13ft (4m) wide, flanked by 'Rusticke pillausters, and sondry mouldings and cornishes' in Portland Stone. In case the next three doorways in the forebuilding should seem inadequate after this tour de force, they were all heightened and new Portland steps were laid.

More difficult to remodel were the four great chambers on the first and second floors. The massive construction of the main walls and the shortage of time prevented anything more elaborate than a hasty refurbishment. Nevertheless, within these limits, there was apparently a remarkable transformation.

New plaster ceilings for the four chambers were constructed by Richard Talbot, the Master Plasterer. The upper floor ones were described as 'archte' – presumably vaulted – and were then painted with a 'frettwoorke in distemper' by the Sergeant Painter to the Court, John de Critz. His talents were also employed in decorating all the cornices to look like stonework (see **colour plate 3b**). Finishing touches were being put in place early in May 1625 when 'new matting diverse rooms and closets' signalled the arrival of the Duke of Buckingham, stopping briefly in Dover on his way to France bearing gifts to Marie de Medici.

The following month, after delays caused by illness and weather, Henrietta Maria disembarked at Dover and lodged in the castle. There, Charles greeted her the next day on his arrival from Canterbury. To a young woman, brought up in one of the most sophisticated and cultured courts in Europe, Dover, despite the frantic attentions lavished on its interior, must have seemed somewhat grim and forbidding. Indeed, one of her entourage, her Chamberlain, later wrote in his memoirs; 'the castle was an old building, constructed in antiquity, where the queen was badly lodged in poorly furnished accommodation, and her companions were treated with scant ceremony, considering the occasion.'

This refurbishing of the keep proved to be something of a swansong for the castle. After Henrietta Maria's stay, it seems to have been quietly recognised that it was no longer possible successfully to adapt for state occasions either the keep or the assortment of medieval buildings surrounding it. Later generations, more keenly aware of antiquities, would be able better to appreciate these. But to the Court officials of the early Stuarts, the buildings probably seemed almost barbaric – their origins lost in the mists of antiquity, their pedigree stretching back to the Saxons, to Arthur and to the Romans. This feeling is apparent in the reaction of the court officials in 1624. Faced with the arrival of Charles's bride, Inigo Jones's staff sought to disguise the rude medieval masonry with triumphal doorways and elaborate plasterwork cunningly painted. A theatrical set, which failed to fool the French visitors.

In 1635, the Office of Ordnance assumed control of all fortifications in England. At Dover, Ordnance officials focussed their attention on the artillery defences around the harbour. Nevertheless, a small garrison seems to have been maintained at the castle. On the outbreak of civil war in 1642 Dover town declared for parliament, but the castle stood by Charles I. This was, however, shortlived. On the night of 21 August 1642, an enterprising and daring merchant, variously named Drake or Daux by later writers, scaled the cliff with eleven armed companions. Once in the castle, they surprised the four guards. Darkness hiding them, the small number of attackers then rounded up the remainder of the garrison of 20 men. The castle had fallen with hardly a shot being fired.

In the Kentish uprising following the execution of Charles I in 1648, the fleet in the Downs joined the rebels, as did the castle garrisons at Deal, Walmer and Sandown. The rebels advanced on Dover and surrounded the castle. The garrison here was commanded by the rabid republican, Sir Algernon Sidney, newly-appointed Governor of Dover. Contemporary reports mention a siege battery thrown up on high ground to the north east, but the advance of Parliamentary forces under Colonel Rich led to its rapid abandonment and the retreat of the rebels to the three castles of the Downs. Dover castle does not appear to have suffered any damage.

Possibly because the castle had been held for Parliament during the civil war, it escaped the slightings meted out to so many royalist strongholds. But although it avoided deliberate destruction, its apparent obsolescence seemed likely to doom it to eventual abandonment. It had a brief renaissance during the euphoria surrounding the Restoration of Charles II in 1660, when it was proposed that the castle and Moat's Bulwark should have a combined garrison of 200 soldiers and gunners. But in June 1661, the garrison was reduced to the Lord Warden, one Gentleman Gunner and 17 gunners, the latter probably concentrated at Moat's Bulwark. Militarily, the castle was perceived to have little use and its prime function by the latter part of the seventeenth century was as official residence for the Warden of the Cinque Ports. Even that ceased in 1708 when the Duke of Dorset obtained the use of Walmer Castle.

Much of the castle must have been disused by 1700, the small garrison and the Lord's

23 *Prisoner-of-war names carved in the keep.*

Wardens' households concentrated on Constable's Tower and some of the buildings of the inner bailey. In the latter, the medieval pentice linking the eastern range with the keep had probably long gone. Elsewhere, the church of St Mary-in-Castro, and its attendant bell-cote in the *pharos*, had probably been little used since the end of the sixteenth century. In 1724, the antiquary William Stukeley noted that the bells had been removed to Portsmouth by Sir George Rooke, the victor of Gibraltar, who had died in 1709. Since then, Stukeley observed: '… the Office of Ordnance, under pretext of savingness, have taken away the lead that covered the tower, and left this rare piece of art and masonry to struggle with the sea air and weather.' It seems probable that the church itself fell into ruin about this time. Only the Cinque Ports', or Debtors' Prison behind Fulbert of Dover's tower preserved something of the former activity within the outer ward. It seems likely that most of the castle outside the walls of the inner bailey was let as grazing land.

In 1689, a report describes the castle as ruinous, its guns useless, but that same year £132 14s 6d was spent fitting it to hold prisoners of war. It seems probable that this money was spent on the keep as the largest secure building. The many carvings by French and other prisoners which can be seen on its walls show that it continued to be a prison well into the eighteenth century. During Marlborough's campaigns around 1500 were incarcerated here (**23**). This use only ceased when the keep was adapted, minimally, to house troops of the castle garrison in the late 1740s.

8

The castle modernised 1740–56

In the late 1730s, political and military events were to cause a rapid re-appraisal of Dover and were to lead to substantial modernisations of the castle and fortifications around the harbour. After the 1740s, defences here were to be strengthened in every subsequent European war in which Britain was involved. Indeed, given the strategic position of the harbour, the

24 *Archcliffe Fort, its seaward bastions demolished by the railway, its landward defences lapped and partly destroyed by the new dual carriageway.*

comparative neglect of Dover's defences in the seventeenth century now seems something of an anomaly.

In the 1730s, the ailing Habsburg empire was causing political instability and fierce rivalries in Europe. By 1739, Spain and Britain were at war. This conflict, reassuringly distant from Britain, was seen as primarily a maritime war. But within five years, Spain had been joined by France. In February 1744, the Brest fleet ostentatiously anchored off Dungeness, causing something of an invasion scare. More

alarmingly Dunkirk was now the centre for preparations for a Jacobite invasion of England. The Brest fleet had been sent to cover this, but a last-minute change caused this particular plan to be abandoned.

Although an invading army could be put ashore on almost any convenient beach, landing heavy artillery and ensuring the regular delivery of supplies and reinforcements demanded a good harbour. Hitler in 1940, Napoleon in 1805 and Marshall Saxe at Dunkirk in 1744 were all aware of this need. More importantly, they all knew that as long as the Royal Navy remained undefeated, their best hope was to use the shortest sea crossing. Good planning and intelligence might allow an invasion when the Royal Navy was elsewhere, while defending a short sea supply route was an easier task than protecting a more extended one. For an invasion force setting out for Britain from northern France or the Low Countries, the obvious target was Dover and its harbour.

25 Moat's Bulwark in 1786. Guilford Battery was to be constructed on the foreshore just beyond it.

These points were not lost on the British government which sought to strengthen the immediate harbour defences from Archcliffe Fort (**24**) to Moat's Bulwark (**25**). The great semi-circular gun battery at the latter fort dates from this invasion scare (**26**). These piecemeal measures were probably sufficent to have ensured that a direct maritime assault on the harbour would have been a costly failure - the record of successful sea-borne assaults on defended harbours was not an encouraging one for any invasion commander.

The alternative for an invader was to capture Dover by landing on the adjacent coast and encircling the town. To the west cliffs made this impossible until beyond Hythe, but to the east, suitable beaches lay beyond Walmer. From either location, a determined force could have marched on Dover in a few hours. Immediately west of the town, Western

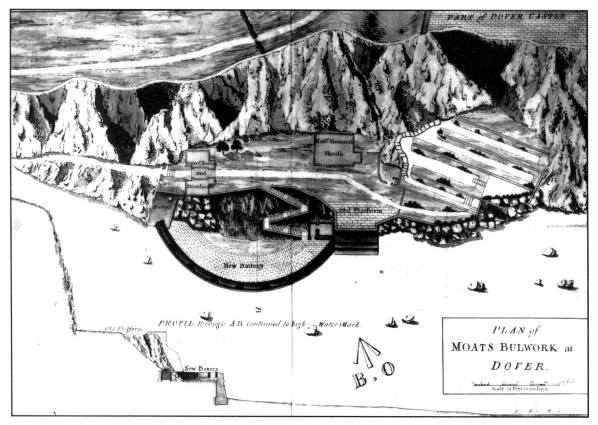

26 *An early eighteenth-century plan of Moat's Bulwark.*

Heights was open downland, while to the east stood the castle. Although outdated in military terms, the castle still presented a formidable problem to an attacker lacking heavy artillery; untaken, it would be impossible to use the harbour. Equally, should the castle and harbour fall, both could prove extremely difficult to recapture unless enemy supply routes across the Channel could be severed. For all these reasons, it was considered imperative to put the castle in good order, not just to resist attack but also to be the base for a body of troops sufficent to contain landings in the vicinity until the main field army could arrive.

Along with strengthening the harbour defences went the need for proper barracks for an enlarged garrison. Since the civil war, there had been widespread resistance to a standing army. In the 1720s, Walpole had run into much opposition when he had proposed raising the peacetime army to 18,000 men. Apart from those posted to coastal forts and castles such as the Tower of London or Dover, the majority of troops were billetted in taverns and private houses. This tended to be unpopular with local communities and did nothing for military discipline and training.

At Dover Castle, construction of a Gunners' Lodging had been authorised in 1732. This was a small two-storey building constructed against the outer curtain south of Constable's Tower. Unlike its contemporary at Walmer Castle, this no longer survives. Neither, however, were barracks for ordinary soldiers. The gunners who occupied these were the small permanent nucleus responsible for the peacetime maintenance of the castle's main armament.

As part of the wartime programme, soldiers' barracks were built at Moat's Bulwark and Archcliffe Fort; none of these survive. However, in 1745 new barracks were begun within the castle's inner bailey (**27**). Along with Ravensdown Barracks at Berwick upon Tweed and barracks at Upnor Castle opposite Chatham, these are among the earliest purpose-built barracks still standing. They incorporate parts of the walls of existing medieval buildings which were by then probably in ruinous condition. Sufficent, however, survived for the Georgian military engineers to incorporate a plaque 'GEORG. II REST. MDCCXLV' on one of the front elevations (**colour plate 8**). Clearly, they regarded their work as adaption rather than complete rebuilding.

The barrack detailing is plain and severe. Officers' quarters are distinguished by round headed windows and, inside, by slightly more generous space. These barracks follow contemporary practice in providing numerous small rooms rather than the large dormitories favoured by the Victorian army. Keep Yard 8 and 9 retain much of their original interiors. The first floor barracks above the former Arthur's Hall were modernised in the third quarter of the nineteenth century and are now one large room. This still has its louvred wooden ventilators, inserted in all barracks following reforms introduced after the Crimean War.

27 *The buildings of the inner bailey.*

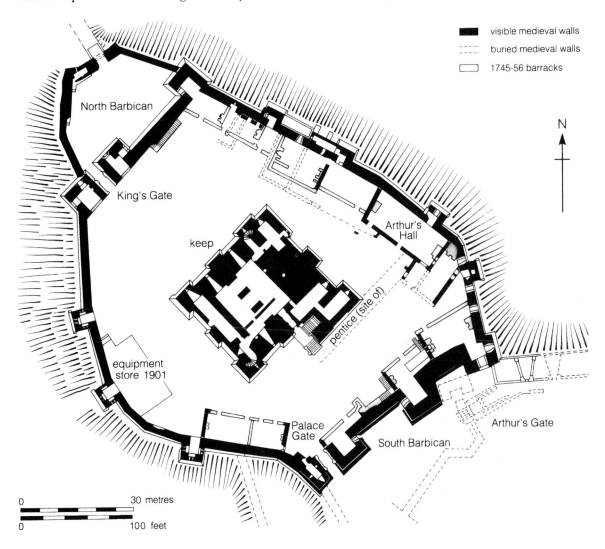

Although these barracks still have their original rainwater hoppers with the date 1745 cast on them, construction and fitting out was probably not completed for around ten years. It is likely that work ceased when peace was declared in 1748. In September 1756, with Britain again at war, J. P. Desmaretz, the engineer then building the great defence lines around Chatham Dockyard, visited Dover. Again, extra troop accommodation was needed in both the town and the castle. Desmaretz reported back to Charles Frederick, Surveyor General to the Board of Ordnance, that:

… as the present barracks are not sufficent to hold one regiment and a half, I have annexed plans and sections and estimates for building, in a slight manner, additional barrack rooms to contain that number; exclusive of half a regiment that may be quartered in the town of Dover.

These additional buildings were single storey, those for privates divided into four rooms each holding 18 men. Officers were more generously housed: four subalterns lived in two rooms, and two captains in four rooms. These may have been sited on flat ground north-west of Colton's Gate.

Desmaretz also looked at the keep, then in use as a storehouse for the Barrack Master. Desmaretz reckoned that the stores could go into the basement, so leaving the first and second floor free. The 'four large rooms with six small ones adjoining' could house 176 men, probably sleeping two to a bed, following the practice of the Georgian army (**28**). By including all existing and potential accommodation in the castle, Archcliffe Fort and Moat's Bulwark, Desmaretz estimated he could house 734 troops; this figure is probably additional to the five companies he reckoned to billet in the 'town and port of Dover'. At that time, the size of a regiment varied considerably. Normally, it was one battalion strong with each battalion having between nine and 13 companies. Each company usually had three sergeants, three corporals and 56 privates

The total estimated cost, including the single storey barracks, an infirmary, storerooms, kitchens, officers' mess and 117 new bedsteads came to £3658. In November 1756, Desmaretz was able to report considerable progress when he wrote to Frederick again:

… the works go on with success and expedition; the barracks within the area of the Keep and the Keep are now completely fitted up for the reception of one battalion, the infirmary and sutler's room [forerunner of the army canteen] are also finished. The two additional barrack rooms at Archcliffe Fort to hold one company will be done this next week, and the new Barrack in Dover Castle for officers and four companies more are proceeded upon with all possible dispatch.

Desmaretz, however, deserves to be remembered as the first engineer to make significant alterations to the defences of the castle for almost 500 years. Within the castle he inherited a number of now-vanished gun batteries, usually constructed of earth with timber revetments. A 1756 report mentions Carter's Gun Battery, Somerset Platform, Five Gun Battery, Monk's Battery, Old Tower, Nine Gun Battery ('an excellent flank for defending the harbour tho' it is upwards of 200 feet above the level of high water'), Three Gun Platform, Seven Gun Battery, North Wall Platform ('which rakes the east shore of the cliff') and two proposed batteries of four and six guns. The nine existing batteries, two of which were at the northern end of the castle, mounted a total of 21 guns, all described as 'unservicable' None of these batteries helped the central problem of how to strengthen the medieval walls to withstand artillery fire.

Like his medieval predecessor Hubert de Burgh, Desmaretz was well aware that the castle was very vulnerable from the high ground to the north east. The mangonels and trebuchets here which faced Hubert in 1216 could only

28 Life in a Georgian barrack room. Terry Ball's reconstruction of a scene inside the barracks completed in 1756. Soldiers slept two to a bed; married men and their wives draped hangings round their beds for a modicum of privacy.

have reached the north-east quadrant of the castle. Twenty-four- or thirty-two-pdr guns in the same location would have raked the entire fortification.

In December 1755, Desmaretz was authorised to strengthen these northern defences and to build two new guard houses. The medieval spur was to be completely remodelled and parapets raised to shield infantry. On the eastern side of the castle a six-gun battery, later named Bell Battery, was to be built between the inner bailey and Penchester Tower (**colour plate 9**). To the south, and firing over it, a four gun battery was to be sited adjacent to St Mary-in-Castro. Both of these batteries were well placed to rake the opposite hillside. To allow them a clear field of fire, the medieval outer curtain between Fitzwilliam Gateway and Avranches Tower was to be reduced in height and strengthened by a massive earth rampart added to its rear.

The records for this work are unusually detailed and provide us with a vivid picture. The garrison soldiers were used for most of the earth-shifting and the reforming of the ramparts; they were supplemented by tradesmen who built the masonry and brickwork. On 18 December 1755 Desmaretz submitted a request for a long list of equipment. This included 200 wheelbarrows, 20 handbarrows, 400 shovels, 200 ballast baskets, 300 pickaxes and 1000 six-inch spikes. On Boxing Day he reported back to his superior officer:

> … I have traced on the ground the capital lines of the intended Covert Way upon the barbican (the medieval spur work) on the north side of this castle; and to prevent any mistakes when on my duty at Chatham, we are now employed in forming (as a model) a small length of the said covert way with its Banquettes, parapet, and the proper talus's for the instruction of the Overseers …

For Desmaretz, Dover must have been something of a side-show compared to his immense works above Chatham. In between his regular visits, he relied heavily on John Bates one of his subordinates at Dover, to drive forward the work and to keep him well-informed. The winter of 1755–6 was notable locally for its driving rain and gales, but despite the appalling weather, good progress was made. The reforming of the northern spur occupied 100 soldiers, two corporals, two sergeants and an officer, who worked daily from 8 a.m. to 4 p.m. In a letter to Desmaretz towards the end of January, Bates reported that the:

> ... parapet to the Round Tower [the present day St John's Tower] which was begun when you were here is nearly completed, and the earth removed to the first Banquette ... The rest of the soldiers employed with outside are removing the earth to form a Terreplein [an earth rampart] between the east and west parapets of the barbican [Spur] towards the exterior point next the Deal Road, and have made tolerable progress in it, but the weather has prevented me from doing much to the east parapet, though it has been stamped out and raised about one foot for near this fortnight; it will be the next work the scavelmen are employed in; and as no timber arrived soon enough to fix the fraizer [sharp poles projecting from the face of a work] in the slope begun when you were here, I was obliged to finish it without them. The rampart within the castle [the outer curtain between Fitzwilliam Gateway and Avranches Tower] opposite the intended six gun battery to the first tower is raised seven feet high and fifty of the soldiers are constantly employed at that work. The masons have have found it a very hard task in pulling down the two towers ... the cement being so very hard that little impression can be made in it ...

Four weeks later, Bates sent in another report:

> We are making what progress we can at the Barbican [Spur], the line fronting the commanding hill [the new rampart between Fitzwilliam and Avranches] and the four gun battery in the church yard; but a Review on Monday and a draught of two additional companies from the regiment has sometimes impeded our works this last week, the inclemency of the weather has greatly added to it ... The glass at the castle barracks is considerably damaged and even some of the stone coping from the hips is blown off ...

Despite these setbacks, four-gun battery was almost finished by the end of March 1756, and six-gun battery was completed in May. Both were armed with 24pdr guns. Opportunity was also taken to re-arm seven of the older earthwork batteries. By early July, the rampart between Fitzwilliam and Avranches was completed with the medieval curtain and mural towers reduced to their present height. The latter had found a further use 'as ... flanks, finding on trial that they were originally hollow and filled up afterwards'.

Completing the spur seems to have taken a little longer, involving several small changes of design at its attenuated tip. Only then were Bates and Desmaretz satisfied that the height and profiles of the ramparts would function properly and provide cover for the troops. The main work was completed by hanging new gates 'at both sally ports as also the entrance of the castle'. The main entrance was Constable's Gateway, the two sally ports may refer to the entrance to the underground tunnel to the Spur and to Fitzwilliam Gateway itself. The latter apparently still had part of its covered way leading to the outer rampart.

When Desmaretz made one of his final tours of inspection in November 1756, construction works were almost complete. He recommended new guard rooms and no less than 20 new sentry boxes. The bleak and exposed conditions here are evident in his order that ten of the sentry boxes were to be 'fixed on wooden frames, with spindils to turn at pleasure, and prevent their being blown down by high winds'. What the unfortunate sentries were to do in these circumstances is not recorded.

1 *An aerial view of the castle from the north west, the keep in the centre. The concentric defences are clearly visible, with the later Great Spur in the foreground. Note the 1940 'dragons teeth' near the tip of the Spur.*

2 *King's Gate, closely protected by its two adjacent towers, and the northern barbican. The bridge from the outer gateway was once connected to the rampart behind the outer curtain wall. Dominating everything is Henry II's keep.*

Dover Castle Great Hall in keep C.1626 Terry Ball. 2.95

3 *a and b Two reconstruction drawings by Terry Ball of the state apartments on the second floor of the keep. On the left is the Great Chamber as it might have appeared soon after completion in the 1180s; the rich decorations are hypothetical. On the right, the same room after hasty modernisation in 1625 for the arrival of Henrietta Maria.*

4 *Troops filing through Colton's Gateway; a watercolour painted in the 1840s.*

5 *The thirteenth-century Fitzwilliam Gateway on the east side of the castle. A vaulted passage once led from the gateway across the bridge and through the outer bank.*

6 *The castle from the east. Henry III's earthwork around the church of St Mary-in-Castro is clearly visible, while inside the inner ward are the roofs and chimneys of the eighteenth-century barracks. Avranches Tower lies to the left of the picture.*

7 *The castle as it probably appeared at the peak of its medieval development towards the end of the thirteenth century. This reconstruction drawing by Terry Ball shows the medieval towers standing to their full height and gives an indication of some of the buildings known to have been within the walls.*

8 *Two of the mid-eighteenth-century barracks on the south side of the inner ward. These are among the oldest barracks in the country.*

9 *Bell Battery, constructed in 1756. Behind it is the site of Four Gun Battery immediately to the north of the church.*

10 *Moat's Bulwark at the foot of the cliff below the castle; a photograph taken from the eighteenth-century gun platform. Ahead lies the earlier gatehouse.*

11 *A reconstruction drawing by Terry Ball showing a meal at the high table in Arthur's Hall in the four-teenth century. Substantial parts of this hall are on view within the later barrack block which stands on the site in the inner ward (copyright English Heritage).*

12 *Looking along the eastern earthworks from the Great Spur. In the foreground is part of the redan of c.1800 with its own ditch protected by firing loops.*

13 *Dover in the early nineteenth century. In the foreground a hay cart crosses the bridge over the Barrier ditch, part of the massive Western Heights fortifications of the Napoleonic wars. Beyond can be seen Archcliffe Fort and in the distance Dover Castle.*

These substantial modifications and strengthening of the castle at its most vulnerable point were the first major works here since the time of Henry III's engineers 500 years earlier. Significantly, they were also the last where the castle was considered almost in isolation. After the middle of the eighteenth century, protecting Dover Harbour was seen as strengthening existing defences and constructing new ones to encircle both town and port.

9

Dover during the
War of American Independence

Between the end of the Seven Years War in 1763 and the begining of the War of American Independence in 1775, the castle relapsed into its peacetime torpor. The garrison was reduced, as was maintenence, the latter to such an extent that in 1771 the curtain between Peverell's Tower and Queen Mary's Tower fell into the ditch after a particulaly wet season. Perhaps to forestall a repeat performance, and to save maintenance costs, the medieval curtain round the top of the earthworks south of St Mary-in-Castro was demolished the following year. Unlike the outer curtain, it had long outlived any military purpose.

When war again broke out with France in 1778, attention was focused on events in America and the West Indies. Nevertheless, home defences were brought to a state of readiness. At the castle, the need for barracks led to proposals to rebuild the ruined church of St Mary-in-Castro and to shift the cooperage and stores there from the keep. Nothing came of this proposal and the church was to remain a ruin for a further eighty years, achieving further ignominy in the interim by being used as a Fives' Court in the early 1790s and then as the garrison coal store during the Napoleonic wars.

In fact, little was done at the castle between 1775 and 1783, save repairs to barracks, construction of a new gunpowder magazine and overhauling the heavy ordnance. Lieutenant (later Captain Sir) Thomas Hyde Page, who was in charge of these works, concentrated resources on defences around the harbour and, for the first time, on Western Heights.

Moat's Bulwark (**colour plate 10**) and Archcliffe Fort were overhauled and their armaments updated, but no significant additions were made to their fabric during this war. They were, however, augmented by additional gun batteries. Adjacent to Moat's Bulwark, the first Guilford Battery was constructed, armed with four 32pdr guns and a number of carronades. Along the waterfront were built a further three detached works, known as North, Townsend and Amherst batteries, all of which had much the same armament (see **71**). With the exception of some of the nineteenth-century buildings associated with Guilford Battery, no trace of any of these now remains.

North's Battery had a particularly short life, apparently abandoned in 1786 as the result of 'an irruption of the sea which destroyed its parapet'. In the Napoleonic wars, nearly £7000 was spent on 'workshops, stores etc.,' here, which suggests that it still had a military use, but it seems to have been demolished a few years later. Townsend's Battery was dismantled in 1843; Amherst's Battery was removed the following year.

The most significant development during this war was the start of fortifications on Western Heights. The need to secure this high ground was obvious. Less apparent was the best way to achieve this without vast expenditure. Lord

Townsend, Master General of Ordnance, clearly took the view that 'field works' – simple earth-work gun batteries – would serve the immediate purpose and would be cheap to construct. These he ordered Page to build. But like other defence projects, before and since, refinements were to transform the enterprise. From this seemingly modest order, probably given in 1780, was to grow the vast brick, stone and earth fortress which in 1823 moved Cobbett to condemn Western Heights as the result of 'either madness the most humiliating, or profligacy the most scandalous'.

We know very little about Page's achievement here. A 1784 plan shows a vast number of works proposed and under construction. On the site of the present Drop Redoubt is an irregular bastionned fort. On the plateau, just before it narrows to a saddleback ridge to the west, is a bastionned work extending the full width of the hilltop and occupying the site of the present citadel. Like the latter, it was clearly intended as a self-contained stronghold. In between these two fortifications are a series of earthwork batteries – presumably the field-works which Townsend had actually asked Page to construct.

By 1784 the only significant progress had been on the south western demi-bastion of the citadel. This was well sited to control the Dover–Folkestone road. A note on the plan records: 'the part ordered in the year 1782 by His Grace the Duke of Richmond to be first erected and upon which the workmen have since been employed'. With the war over in 1783, work tailed off rapidly, but not before the whole scheme had been marked on the hilltop. In the summer of 1787, a Lieutenant Hay visited the Heights and reported that although the works were very incomplete, he had 'traced their general outline and marked them on the survey'. Even in their unfinished state, they attracted critics. In 1790's Lord Torrington stayed in Dover and recorded:

> Our evening ramble was a survey of the Moat's Bulwark, a seemingly unnecessary charge; but not a tenth part so ridiculous as The Battery Upon The Hill, built by an engineer (a quondam acquaintance of mine), for the purpose, only, of pillaging the State.

These were harsh words, but remained in the privacy of the writer's diary until publication much later. The fortifications at Dover undertaken during the War of American Independence were substantial. They were however, little more than a prelude, a curtain raiser to the colossal construction projects here during the Napoleonic wars from 1793 to 1815.

10
The castle during the Napoleonic Wars

War with Revolutionary France broke out in 1793. Probably nobody forsaw that hostilities were to last, save for short intermissions, for over twenty years. With the two most powerful states in Europe confronting each other across the Channel, one supreme at sea, the other with its citizen armies seemingly invincible on land, the strategic importance of Dover needed no emphasis in military and political minds. Between 1793 and 1815 probably around half a million pounds was spent on the town's and harbour's fortifications, giving them much of their present appearance. The castle itself had nearly £80,000 spent modifying and augmenting defence works begun nearly 40 years before. This time, the military engineers had backing at the highest level and funds to match. No other fortifications in Britain had anything approaching such sums spent on them during these wars.

In 1798, Viscount Melville, Secretary of State for War, drew up a memorandum on the defence of southern England, supposing it to be threatened by a French invasion:

In this state of things, the importance of Dover Castle and Sandown [Castle] exceed calculations. They are well fortified, should be well provided, well commanded, and not taken by assault. Without Dover Castle the enemy can have no certain communication; and always supposing that on our shore he finds no means to advance his purpose, the bringing up and placing suffcient artillery to reduce it is a work of slow process and would give time to relieve it, whether he remained in east Kent and made that his chief object or whether he found himself sufficently strong to press on to the Medway and there wait the result, if in the meantime he could depend upon subsisting in the country.

The possession to an enemy of Dover Castle and of the opposite entrenched [Western] Height and of the town and port, fortified in the mannner in which he would soon accomplish and defended by 6 or 7,000 men would establish a sure communication with France and could not be easily wrested from his hands. The conquest of this alone would be to him a suffcient object could he arrive with means of immediately attacking it. Its preservation to us is most important …

A French invasion, however, did not become a real threat until the resumption of hostilities in 1803. For the next two years, Napoleon's main aim was the invasion and defeat of Great Britain. Across the Straits, three army corps were camped on the clifftops near Boulogne, while from Etaples round to Ostend shipwrights were busy constructing flat-bottomed barges while officials assembled an armada of fishing boats and other small craft. By early 1805, Napoleon had invasion shipping for almost 168,000 troops and their equipment.

The year before he had said, 'Let us be masters of the Straits for six hours,' adding, with more confidence than modesty, 'and we shall be masters of the world.'

But Napoleon, like Hitler 140 years later, first had to contend with the Royal Navy. While the Channel Fleet, under Admiral Cornwallis, cruised the western approaches and kept guard on the French naval bases at Brest and Rochefort, Admiral Lord Keith's squadrons patrolled east from Selsey Bill into the waters of the North Sea. Backed by the best-equipped dockyards in Europe, the British fleet was able to blockade closely the French ports. Their weatherbeaten cruising squadrons were all too visible, both to the Grand Army and to the invasion flotillas.

Such disciplined use of sea power was very imperfectly understood by most people. Almost alone in 1804, the Admiralty remained largely unmoved by fears of invasion: in the House of Lords, the First Lord of the Admiralty, St Vincent, sought to reassure his fellow peers. 'I do not say, my Lords', he observed, 'that the French will not come. I only say that they will not come by sea.' Something of this same insouciance was also apparent among some of the inhabitants of Dover. On clear days, Napoleon's army camp was just visible above Boulogne to those citizens with telescopes. Others preferred to investigate more closely. Thomas Pattenden noted in his diary for 1 August 1804:

Yesterday, my neighbour Mr Squier went with some officers of the militia here in a cutter to see Boulogne … where they remained long enough to see and satisfy themselves with the sight of the camps etc., …

Four weeks later, Mr Squier 'went a second time with a party to Boulogne', but the following day, boldness was nearly his undoing:

Mr Squier returned home this morning from Boulogne. The Gentlemen that hired the cutter requested the Master to take them off the harbour of Calais, which he did, and they very imprudently exposed themselves to great danger, being fired on very often by the Batterys, and might have been easily taken prisoners if the French had manned a boat …

But however confident the Admiralty and the bolder citizens of Dover might be in the Navy's capacity to thwart an invasion, most people were not so sure. As long as ships depended on sails, wind was a key factor. *God breathed and they were scattered,* ran the inscription on one of the medals Elizabeth I had struck to commemorate the defeat of the Spanish Armada. A century later, in 1688, an easterly wind – the 'Protestant Wind' – had trapped the Royal Navy off the Gunfleet Shoal south of the Thames estuary while driving William's fleet past it to an unopposed landing in Devon. In the early nineteenth century, this event was still remembered, and who could tell where God's sympathies now lay? There was also a chance that a French fleet might escape from Brest unnoticed, sail up the Channel and secure the Straits just long enough to allow the French army to cross to England. Such a possibility was outlined by Admiral Keith to the Duke of York, Commander-in-Chief of the army, in October 1803. Indeed, the admiral's assessment bore considerable similarities to Napoleon's orders to Admiral Villeneuve in the Spring of 1805.

Given the imponderables of sea power, no wartime British government could neglect its secondary defences, least of all at the port most likely to be target of a French invasion. This policy held good throughout the war, even when Napoleon had formally abandoned invasion plans and marched his Grand Army away.

From 1792 to 1809 Lieutenant Colonel William Twiss, one of the most able and experienced military engineers of his generation, was in charge of the works at Dover. Promoted to be Colonel-Commandant of the Royal Engineers in 1809, he continued to exercise control, although day-to-day supervision was provided by Captain William Ford. Although a much younger man, he had considerable experience and was also closely involved in the design, siting and construction of the chain of Martello Towers being erected along the southern coastline of Kent and eastern Sussex between 1805 and 1812. These two men had more impact on the defences of Dover than any military engineers since the time of Henry II and Henry III.

At the castle, most of the improvements to the defences took place between 1794 and 1805; minor works, however, continued to the end of the wars. By 1795, the scale of operations was such that Twiss was given the help of four assistant engineers. Late that summer over 1200 men were at work in the Dover district. By June 1797, 29 carpenters at the castle were constructing traversing carriages and gun platforms, a portcullis and floors and centering for casemates and guardrooms. Thirty masons were busy repairing the medieval walls and paving a new entrance (Canon's Gate). Several hundred men of the East Suffolk and Montgomery militias were helping with the repair work, creating new ramparts and deepening ditches. The scale of these latter operations is indicated by the employment of 70 men from the Royal Artillery Drivers 'attending carts and wagons in moving ground and transporting materials'.

The main effort was again concentrated on the vulnerable eastern side of the castle which was most likely to bear the brunt of a besieging force. Here, Desmaretz in the 1750s had reformed the outer defences north from Avranches Tower. His successor, Twiss, concentrated on the largely unmodernised medieval circuit running south to the cliff edge (see **21** and **colour plate 11**)

The work of the 1790s followed that of 40 years before. Surviving medieval towers were reduced in height and a massive chalk and earth rampart was constructed against the medieval curtain wall. New gun positions on

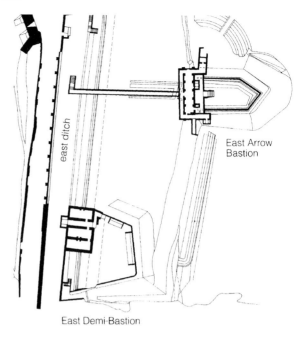

east ditch

East Arrow Bastion

East Demi-Bastion

29 *East Arrow and East Demi-Bastions.*

the rampart were serviced by two gun ramps to the rear. The ditch itself was dramatically widened and deepened and where the chalk proved unstable, brick revetments were built. An extra gun battery apparently was sited just to the north of St Mary-in-Castro, augmenting the four-gun battery installed here in the 1750s.

With more resources than Desmaretz, who had concentrated on modernising the existing line of medieval wall, Twiss extended the defences outside this circuit. Beyond the reformed counterscarp, or outer bank, he placed four powerful outworks, their guns designed to sweep the hill slopes below the castle. These outworks were lower than the main rampart behind, enabling guns on the latter to fire over them to the hillside beyond. By this means, a criss-cross of gunfire could sweep the ground east of the castle. East of Avranches Tower Twiss built the massive Horseshoe Bastion. South-east of this, at the salient angle of the medieval curtain, he placed Hudson's Bastion and south of that, near the cliff edge, he raised East Demi-Bastion. Further down the hillside below Hudson's and East Demi-

Bastion, was constructed the detached East Arrow Bastion.

As these outworks were forward of the main defences, Twiss planned their communications very carefully. Horseshoe, Hudson's and East Demi-Bastion were each approached by their own separate underground passages entered from behind the main east rampart. These three also had doorways, heavily protected by small drawbridges and firing loops, which led directly into the east ditch. In the 1850s, the approach to Hudson's Bastion was to be altered substantially by a caponier, but the others remain much as completed by Twiss. Horseshoe Bastion, the largest of these detached works, contains a substantial vaulted chamber to its rear. In its rear wall is a blocked doorway and traces of a drawbridge. On either side of the doorway are firing loops, while a small gallery on the eastern side provided enfilading fire. No evidence survives to indicate

whether the drawbridge was part of a bridge to the main rampart, or whether it merely led to a set of steps to the moat as with some of the near-contemporary Martello towers. The vaulted chamber may be the 'bomb proof barrack for forty five men in peace or 150 during a siege' referred to by Twiss in a letter in June 1803, the month after Britain had renewed war against Napoleonic France.

East Arrow Bastion, further to the east, was in effect a detached work and potentially more vulnerable (**29**). For security, its communication tunnel led to the bottom of the main ditch and not into the interior of the castle.

While this work was going on, Twiss also sought to improve the spur defences at the northern tip of the castle (**colour plate 12**).

30 *Looking north to the Spur. In the foreground is St John's Tower and beyond it the caponier linking Spur and Redan.*

31 *The upper gallery in the caponier leading to the Underground Works, its embrasures covering the northern end of the moat.*

Here the need remained to dominate the higher ground to the north. In August 1801 he recorded progress in a letter to the Lord Warden, William Pitt:

> ... early this war we raised within it a sort of Redan which seems to answer many good purposes and this year we have further improved this Redan by sinking a small ditch in front of it ...

The ditch needed a revetment wall and the defences here were to be completed by 'a bomb-proof guardroom and passages and hanging doors with a proper drawbridge for its security ...' In June 1803 Twiss recorded that these 'and bomb-proof defences before each shoulder ... are going on as fast as we can' (**30**).

This correspondence conveys little of Twiss's remarkable alterations here. The redan, or raised gun battery on top of the spur, was a standard military solution to the problem of siting guns at a higher level. What was unique were the quite extraordinary arrangements for local communication and defence. The approach to the spur from the castle followed the medieval route, but crossed the ditch from

St John's Tower through the lower level of a two-tier caponier (**31**, **32**). At its northern end a heavy falling door, controlled from the upper level, could be dropped to deny access to the passage if enemy soldiers had entered the spur.

Within the spur itself, the three medieval passages, which originally had fanned out to sally ports, had been largely destroyed, probably by Desmaretz in the 1750s (**33**). Where they now ended, Twiss constructed a new route down to a small sally-port on the south western flank of the spur. This was overlooked by musket loops and a guard-room from where iron levers operated inner and outer doors (**34**). The outer door emerged into the ditch to the rear of the spur; the inner door could be set to divert any unwelcome intruders into a tiny courtyard overlooked by firing positions. Seldom has the ingenuity of military engineers been better displayed than in these elaborate arrangements, designed to allow raiding parties and castle guards out, and prevent hostile troops entering. Later, Victorian

32 *A cross-section of the caponier of the Underground Works showing it in its early nineteenth-century form.*

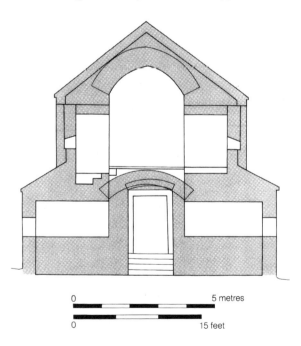

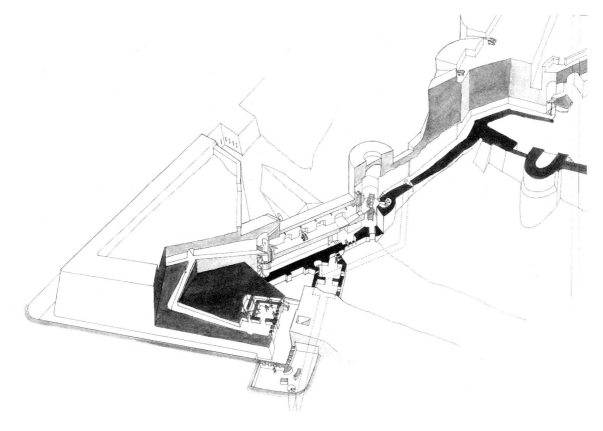

military engineers were to add counterscarp galleries to the redan, but what remains today is essentially what Twiss and his assistants completed in 1803.

Although the bulk of expenditure on the castle was to improvements on its eastern side, Twiss made important additions on the west. Documentary sources are largely silent, but it seems that it was he who reduced all the mural towers south of Constable's Tower, except for Peverell's Tower, to their present height and added an earth and chalk rampart behind the medieval curtain south from Gatton's Tower (see **18**). Much of the rampart material probably came from deepening the ditch. Although there was a firing step, no provision was made for artillery as the hillside falls away steeply to the valley below. It is possible that mortars may have been proposed as heavy weapons here. Immediately outside and a little below the counterscarp of the deepened medieval ditch, Twiss formed a second rampart for

33 *A cut-away illustration of the Underground Works, showing them in their final elaborate early nineteenth-century arrangement* (drawing by Terry Ball).

34 *The guardroom in the Underground Works. The iron levers control doors leading outside.*

troops to command the road from the town. At the southern end, this rampart joined a shallow bastion, forming part of the protection to Canon's Gate. A small tunnel led under the outer bank of the medieval moat to a vertical brick shaft behind the new outer rampart. This gave soldiers secure communication, via a new caponier and sally-port under Constable's Tower, enabling them to reach the outer defences without exposing themselves to enemy fire.

To provide enfilading fire along the western face of the defences, and to give a measure of protection to troops manning the western ramparts to the south of it, Twiss constructed a large blunt-ended bastion south west of Constable's Gateway (see **1**). Four guns on traversing carriages were positioned to cover the north western approaches to the castle.

Although there had been some form of medieval sally port near the southern end of the west curtain, Constable's Gateway remained the main access to the castle. It was however, inconveniently sited for rapid communication with the town and harbour. In the mid 1790s, Twiss began a major reconstruction to remedy this. South from Rokesley's Tower to the cliff the medieval curtain was largely torn down. Apart from maintaining its line, the military engineers kept little else, save for the Tudor bulwark which had a residual use providing enfilading fire along the ditch. Immediately south of Rokesley's Tower, Twiss constructed the strongly defended Canon's Gateway, a vaulted bomb-proof passage with twin doors. Wide enough to take a column of troops, this was approached by a road from the present Castle Hill road. This was covered by the new outer defences, before entering a barbican and crossing the ditch on a drawbridge above a caponier (**35**).

Immediately south of Canon's Gateway were built five casemates; the northern one, communicating directly with the gate passage, became the guard room. All these were nearing completion in June 1797 when masons were

35 *Canon's Gateway, completed in 1797. Note the two-tier caponier beneath the bridge and the wall of the Tudor bulwark in the ditch beyond.*

paving the gate passage. Canon's Gateway greatly speeded communications between town and castle.

Within the castle, Twiss also sought to improve access and remove obsolete parts of the defences. It was now that the medieval walls in the vicinity of Harcourt's Tower were finally removed along with remains of a ditch there. The local historian, John Lyon, sadly noted that:

… in the year 1797 the demolishing hand of the modernising engineer put the finishing strokes … and the end of the interior ditch at the place [Harcourt's Tower] is filled up to make a way for carriages from the vallum across the quadrangle to the new well [at the end of the spur road up to Palace Gate (see **7**)].

To the regret of Lyon and also of subsequent medieval historians, the heart of the castle did not escape this remorseless modernisation. The roofs were stripped from Henry II's keep and two massive brick vaults were inserted above the state chambers on the second floor. These were partly to 'bomb-proof' the building and protect it from plunging mortar-fire, but mainly to enable heavy guns to be mounted on the roof. Traces of their traversing mountings still remain. These guns provided a valuable 'third tier' of artillery at the northern end of the fortifications (see **5**).

By 1800, if Statham's figures are accurate, a total of around 200 heavy weapons were mounted within the castle. These included 74 guns of various calibres from 18 to 32pdr, 28 mortars, four 10in howitzers, 44 carronades, 10 amusettes – light, long-barrelled field guns – and around 50 wall-pieces, small guns mounted on brackets on the walls.

Not surprisingly, accommodation for the garrison for all these extra fortifications and weapons was at a premium. Keep Yard barracks were fully occupied and much of Twiss' time was devoted to finding more space, either for temporary hutted accommodation or for more permanent quarters. Four of the casemates adjacent to Canon's Gateway were designed as barracks; John Lyon mentions other 'barracks, a bakehouse, kitchen and a magazine, all of Masterly Workmanship' in the vicinity. With the exception of the magazine and the casemates, these have all long gone.

The magazine was built just to the north of Canon's Gate. It is of brick, of conventional vaulted construction and held 320 powder barrels (**36**). Probably contemporary with it is a

36 *The powder magazine of* c.*1800 near Canon's Gate. The protective earth bank is an addition of some 50 years later.*

much larger powder magazine, now buried, which exists west of the Officers' Mess. This magazine was originally known as 'Long Gun Magazine' after Queen Elizabeth's Pocket Pistol which then stood nearby (see **22**). A plan of 1810 noted that this held 864 powder barrels, while a further magazine within the castle to the west of Hudson's Bastion also held 320 barrels.

Between 1801 and 1803, Twiss was to propose further casemates. These apparently included those which still remain under the ramparts south of Bell Battery – though these may not have been built until some years later – and those to the rear of the Norfolk Towers. These latter had gun positions above them, firing north over the Spur. In November 1805, Twiss wrote to Morse:

I would recommend that Mr Trimmer be employed in finding earth near Dover Castle for about 500,000 bricks to be made in 1806, by way of experiment, because I think it advisable eventually to build more casemates for troops and stores in Dover Castle …

Contemporary plans show ground north-west of Colton's Tower covered in barracks, with more north of Canon's Gateway on the site now occupied by the Royal Garrison Artillery Barracks of 1912. A little way in from the cliff edge stood a military hospital.

The garrison probably reached a peak during these wars. Such a concentration of troops demanded adequate water supplies and sanitation if deseases and epidemics were to be avoided. By then, the medieval well within the keep appears to have been disused and partly infilled. In the 1790s, military engineers sank a new well midway between Colton's Gate and Palace Gate. This was convenient for both the barracks in the immediate vicinity and those in Keep Yard. It rapidly took over from the other two wells within the castle as the main source of water and about 1800 was covered with a

'bomb proof' brick vault as protection from bombardment. This remains a prominent feature, later in the nineteenth-century housing a steam pump.

Sanitation here had probably advanced little since the time of Henry II. Those medieval garderobes which discharged directly into the ditches may have been abandoned, but the garrison still relied on privies draining into cesspits. Such may have been adequate for a small peacetime garrison, but the numbers of troops now made better arrangements imperative. In 1807 and 1808, substantial sums were spent 'forming a system of drains from Dover Castle to the sea'. Details are lacking, but these in all probability joined the oval brick drain, part of which still survives, tunnelled through the cliff to connect the latrines of the Underground Barracks with the sea.

Along with these improvements went new rules for the garrison. Most of the 20 Dover Castle Barrack Regulations issued in December 1799 and 'fixed up conspicuously in the Barrack Rooms of each Regiment' have a very modern ring, emphasising the need to keep rooms and passages clean and the insistence on bedding being rolled up each morning. Men ate in messes of twelve and their rooms were inspected each month by the senior officers. 'Any man having symptons of the Itch, or other infections' had to be sent to the garrison hospital; while 'No Woman is to be permitted to wash in any part of the Barrack Rooms.'

In his history of Dover, written towards the end of the Napoleonic Wars, John Lyon records the crammed space within the southern part of the castle:

The far greater part of the ground on the side of the Castle Hill, next the cliff, has either been covered with magazines and other buildings, parks for shot, mounds of earth, and ventilators made for casemates in the front of the cliff, for lodging the soldiers, that an engineer in future will find it extremely difficult to find a vacant place for a redoubt or a bastion …

This reference to the cliff casemates is virtually the only contemporary mention of perhaps the most extraordinary 'barracks' ever constructed in Britain. In 1797, faced with the almost impossible task of finding further space to house troops in the castle, the military authorities adopted a radical solution. Teams of miners

began excavating in from the cliff face to provide underground accommodation (**37**).

By then, the Royal Engineers had experience excavating extensive tunnels for gun emplacements within the Rock of Gibraltar during the Great Siege (1779–83). At Chatham, they had also constructed a considerable network of tunnels below Fort Amherst. These in part were

37 *A plan of the Underground Barracks.*

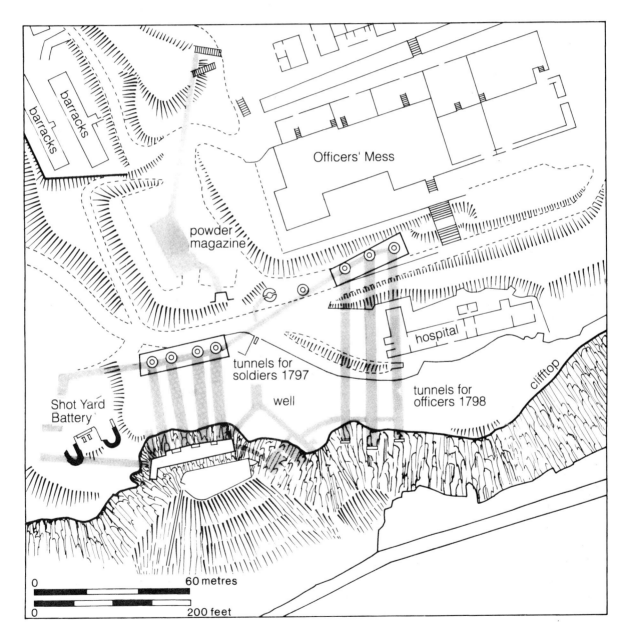

communication tunnels, but they also housed guns overlooking Barrier Ditch and provided living quarters for the guns' crews. Twiss would have been well aware of these and it is probable that the Dover underground barracks were his idea.

Underground barracks at Dover had several advantages apart from saving space at ground level. The chalk subsoil was easy to excavate and was largely self-supporting. It was comparatively easy to cut an entrance ramp from a point near Canon's Gateway and above all else, the tunnels were safe. Their entrances were too high up the cliff to be at risk from bombardment by warships, and they would have been totally impervious to any landward artillery barrage (**38**).

38 *The cliff front of the Underground Barracks.*

39 *Garrison Life inside one of the cliff Underground Barracks* c.*1810. Men ate and slept here, their muskets stacked in racks and their possessions above their beds* (drawing by Terry Ball).

In 1797, four parallel tunnels or 'subterraneous bombproofs' were excavated in from the cliff face a distance of 100ft (around 30m) as accommodation for soldiers. The following year, a further group of three larger and longer tunnels were sited to the east of these for officers. Between the two groups were dug a well and latrines, linked by a communication tunnel. To the rear of the accommodation tunnels, a further passage or 'gallery of communication' led to a second entrance within the castle a little way in from the cliff. This rear passage may be a slightly later addition: in the summer of 1803, Twiss was proposing 'more communication opened to them' because of the number of troops then quartered there (see **37**).

All the tunnels had fireplaces, their flues cut through the chalk. Ventilation was provided at the head of each of the seven main accommodation tunnels and midway along the rear communication passage by constructing eight sizable vertical shafts to the ground above. The seaward ends of the tunnels had brick fronts with doors and windows for access and light. Evidence suggests that the four tunnels for soldiers may have had first floors inserted later, approached by staircases midway along the two outer tunnels.

Ease of excavation enabled the tunnels to be completed by the end of 1798. Early in 1799 though, there was a serious fall of chalk near the well. In the winter of 1806, a major fall 'entirely cut off all communication in front of

these casemates', and again in November 1810 a large portion of the cliff face collapsed. Probably as a consequence of the first fall, the barrack tunnels were brick-lined, this work being completed in 1810.

By the summer of 1803, the first troops had occupied these new quarters (**39**). Regrettably, no contemporary accounts have been found of life in these strange underground barracks. The few fireplaces would have provided only limited warmth, while for light the occupants must have been largely dependent on lanterns. Records show that troops were provided with iron bedsteads, considered more hygenic than wooden ones. An 1812 account refers to 'several underground barracks, particularly the Royal Billy … where one room will contain 500 men'. If accurate, this suggests that around 2000 soldiers plus officers could have lived underground.

Despite all this military activity and the ceaseless construction work, aspects of the castle's peacetime life continued. The residual business of the Cinque Ports continued here, as did the Cinque Ports' prison, which lies to the rear of Fulbert of Dover's Tower and was by then normally only used by a few debtors. In 1796, the Board of Ordnance enlarged it by adding three rooms and an exercize yard (**40**). The latter was only 25ft by 50ft (7.5m by 15m),

40 *The Debtors' Prison, with its exercize yard to the south, c.1830.*

latrine

walled exercise yard

prison

0   10 metres
0   30 feet

its walls so high that, according to Lyon, 'the rays of the sun cannot reach the bottom, and it is cold and damp in winter'. It lay immediately south of the prison, bounded by the medieval curtain on its west side and with a double privy at its southern end. Although the prison was taken over in 1798 by the Barrack Department, this was apparently a short-lived change, probably because it was too small and cramped for use by soldiers. Interestingly, even in wartime visitors still came to the castle, for Lyon records that 'there is a grating for the prisoners to look through, in the second storey of the building, where they can let down the purse to receive the contributions of visitors in their walks round the castle'.

If these visitors came to see the keep, they would have found its external appearance very different from now. When first built in the 1180s, it was probably rendered, but this would not have lasted long. However, in 1808, Twiss related:

> Captain Ford reports to me that the casing of masonry, which was put up against the wall of the old KEEP in DOVER CASTLE, about 50 years ago, and which has during many years past been falling down in pieces, has lately come down in such quantities, as to excite general alarm amongst the

troops, and rendered it absolutely necessary for the safety of the garrison to take the whole of this casing down, which has been done without accident.

> After many consultations respecting the best mode of securing the OLD KEEP, I some years ago inserted in the annual Estimates the sum of £329-16-9d for covering the surface with Parker's Cement and I am still of the opinion it is the best mode of preserving it that can be adopted, the sole object being to render the surface so smooth that the wet may not hang upon it, by that means avoiding most of the mischief done by the frost ...

Permission for the work was obtained from the Board of Ordnance, and there is no reason to doubt that it was carried out. Parker's Cement, a patent waterproof cement, was invented in 1796 using septaria from the Isle of Sheppey. It would have made the keep into something ressembling a large dark brown concrete block. However, the earliest photographs of the keep show little evidence of it, suggesting that it was no longer-lived than any of its predecessors (see **8**).

By 1810, the interior of the keep was a huge gunpowder magazine; each of the two upper floors had space for 3990 powder barrels, while the basement held a further 800.

11
Western Heights and harbour defences 1793–1815

On the outbreak of war in 1793, modernisation of the castle's defences was given priority. In the first three war years, the £5000 spent on Western Heights suggests little more than a modest refurbishment and repair of those parts of the defences which Lieutenant Page had completed more than ten years earlier. Expenditure then ceased entirely until 1804.

Around the harbour, small sums were spent repairing Archcliffe Fort and North's Battery and, although they are not specifically mentioned, we can assume that Moat's Bulwark, Guilford and Amherst's Batteries would all have been brought into a state of readiness (see **71**). Very often, the biggest expenditure was provision of new gun carriages to replace those which had rotted from standing in the open.

When war resumed in May 1803, there was very real fear of a French invasion. For the next three years, Dover was the scene of frantic activity and, although this lessened after 1805, work on the defences was pressed ahead to the very end of the war. At the outset, the main concern was to ensure that all available guns were provided with mounts and carriages. In June Twiss reported that 'seventeen traversing platforms are yet wanting between Dover Castle and Hythe Bay'. A shortage of timber was preventing manufacture of these, but 'several ships with timber are expected from the Baltic' – another instance of the vital importance which the government and the Royal Navy attached to keeping the Baltic trade routes open.

Although attention was to be focused on Western Heights, considerable time and energy were expended on the harbour level fortifications. Captain Ford, probably mindful of similar schemes for Romney Marsh, spent some time fruitlessly investigating whether the River Dour could be used to flood the town in the event of invasion. Existing fortifications were brought to a state of readiness. New palisades were recommended for the ditch of Guilford Battery, and new flank defences, armed with three 12pdr guns, were constructed at Archcliffe Fort. By April 1804, a new redoubt on the site of the ruined Townsend's Battery was nearing completion. This was linked to a line of palisades – the military forerunner of barbed wire entanglements – along the front. Early in the war, Admiral Lord Keith, whose warships were blocading the French invasion ports, inspected the harbour defences and pressed for a boom or chain to close the harbour mouth as a protection against raids. Although proposals were drawn up, it is not certain whether a boom was ever installed. In the spring of 1804, shortly before becoming Prime Minister, William Pitt paid several visits to Dover and walked the defences with Captain Ford, who had 'to explain to him what was to be done'. Finishing touches to the harbour level defences were being completed in May 1808 when Captain Ford began construction of a guard house and couvre port, or outwork to protect the entrance to Archcliffe Fort.

Shortly after the resumption of the war, the Duke of York, Commander-in-Chief of the army, wrote to General Sir David Dundas, then commanding the Southern District, and asked him to consider extra security measures for Dover, including stationing a reserve corps of between five and six thousand men there to counter any enemy landings. Dundas and Twiss then spent two days examining Western Heights. Twiss felt very strongly that 'the public

service might be greatly benefitted if these Heights could be kept possession of by detached Redoubts with small garrisons ...' In his report to Dundas, he did not favour stationing a corps there as existing field works were inadequate protection and there was no water supply. However, Twiss ended by writing:

... I do not conceive that this opinion militates against the idea of occupying Dover Heights with a respectabe fortress or by several detached redoubts well revetted ...

41 *A plan of the fortifications on Western Heights.*

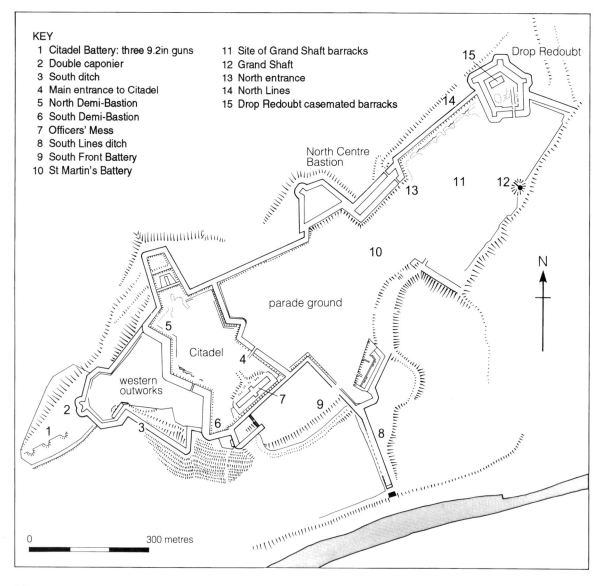

KEY
1 Citadel Battery: three 9.2in guns
2 Double caponier
3 South ditch
4 Main entrance to Citadel
5 North Demi-Bastion
6 South Demi-Bastion
7 Officers' Mess
8 South Lines ditch
9 South Front Battery
10 St Martin's Battery
11 Site of Grand Shaft barracks
12 Grand Shaft
13 North entrance
14 North Lines
15 Drop Redoubt casemated barracks

Drop Redoubt

North Centre Bastion

parade ground

Citadel

western outworks

0   300 metres

N

Although favourably received by the Duke of York and the Earl of Chatham, who was Master of the Ordnance and William Pitt's elder brother, the complexities, scale and likely cost of such a project ensured that almost a year passed in technical discussions over the actual design.

Finally, in April 1804, Lieutenant-General Robert Morse, Inspector General of Fortifications, authorised Twiss to proceed and to make use of 'the existing imperfect works' to form a citadel at the western end. This was to remain largely a 'field work' as envisaged in the War of American Independence. At the lower eastern end, where the ground falls precipitously to the harbour and town, Twiss was to build a powerful irregular polygonal fort – Drop Redoubt. A deep defensive ditch was to link the two along the northern scarp of the hill. Midway along was to be a substantial independent work called North Centre Bastion. These works were to be casemated for troop acommodation. Much of the hill along its southern flank was too steep to warrant fortifications. Morse estimated the total cost – 'half of which may be considered as for barracks' – at £30,000. It was not one of the army's more accurate financial forecasts (**41**).

Throughout the summer of 1804 excellent progress was made. For Twiss and his senior staff, such as Captain William Ford, this was a time of frantic activity. Their responsibilities for fortifications meant that much of their time was spent on horseback travelling along the southern coast of Kent and east Sussex inspecting defence works. By 1804 there were no less than 15 fortifications of varying sizes between Folkestone and Lydd. Further west, the low-lying area of the Pevensey Levels was protected by a further 19-gun batteries, while inland, river crossings at places such as Newenden, Bodiam and Robertsbridge were guarded by small batteries. Part of the summer of 1804 was spent by Twiss surveying the coast from Beachy Head to Dover for sites for the proposed chain of guntowers. The design and siting of these, soon to

be known as Martello towers, involved the engineers in corrospondence and meetings in Rochester and Chatham. Not the least of their tasks was securing the huge quantities of building materials needed for all these works. Huge quantities of bricks, mostly from the London brickfields, had to be ordered and transported round the coast.

In May 1804, Pitt returned as Prime Minister. Keenly interested in defences here – as Lord Warden he had spent much time at Walmer Castle – he spurred on the work. In September, he added to the Royal Engineers' tasks by authorising construction of the Royal Military Canal, a defensible waterway to run from Hythe to the river Rother and cut off Romney Marsh from the high ground to the north. All the while, reports from France of invasion preparations gave an added urgency.

A major problem for Twiss at Western Heights was that of access. With new barracks on the Heights, it was essential that troops could travel rapidly from there to the town and defences below. As Twiss wrote to Morse in the early autumn of 1804 when bad weather was becoming imminent:

> the new barracks … are little more than 300 yards [274m] horizontally from the sea beach … and about 180 feet [54.8m] above high water mark, but in order to communicate with them from the centre of the town, on horseback the distance is nearly a mile and a half and to walk it about threequarters of a mile, and all the roads unavoidably pass over ground more than 100 feet [30m] above the barracks, besides the footpaths are so steep and chalky that a number of accidents will unavoidably happen during the wet weather and more especially after floods.

These barracks were to accommodate 700 men (**42**); a further 800 were to be quartered in casemate accommodation in the actual fortifications on the Heights, as well as staff for a military

hospital for the Royal Artillery. This last was certainly in use by 1810, when Dover as a whole had barracks for 3000 soldiers. These figures ignore the troops in tented accommodation and billeted in town. The ability to move large bodies of troops swiftly to reinforce areas of the defences in the event of attack made good communications of paramount importance. A new road to link town and Heights would have seemed an obvious solution, but Twiss favoured a far bolder course (**43**):

> ... I am ... induced to recommend the construction of a shaft, with a triple staircase ... the chief object of which is the convenience and safety of troops ... and may eventually be useful in sending reinforcements to troops or in affording them a secure retreat.

From the new barracks on the Heights, Twiss proposed a flight of steps be cut into the hillside to a circular shaft 26ft (7.9m) in diameter and 140ft (42.6m) deep. From the bottom of this shaft a 180ft (54.8m) gallery through the

42 Looking across Grand Shaft Barracks to the castle. Grand Shaft can be seen near bottom right, part of Drop Redoubt top left. A pre-war photograph.

chalk led directly to Snargate Street. He estimated the whole cost at less than £4000. Permission was forthcoming and by March 1805 only 40ft (12m) of the gallery remained to be excavated and it seems probable that Grand Shaft was in use by 1807.

The shaft comprises two vertical brick cylinders, one inside the other, the inner cylinder pierced by a series of round-headed openings taking light from the central light well. Between the two cylinders are three concentric spiral staircases on brick arches, originally with Purbeck stone treads (**44**). Columns of troops, six abreast, could use Grand Shaft without needing to reform. It is a bold and imaginative solution to a particular problem, and it remains a singular piece of military engineering. Grand Shaft is a fitting memorial to William Twiss, and the skills of the Royal Engineers.

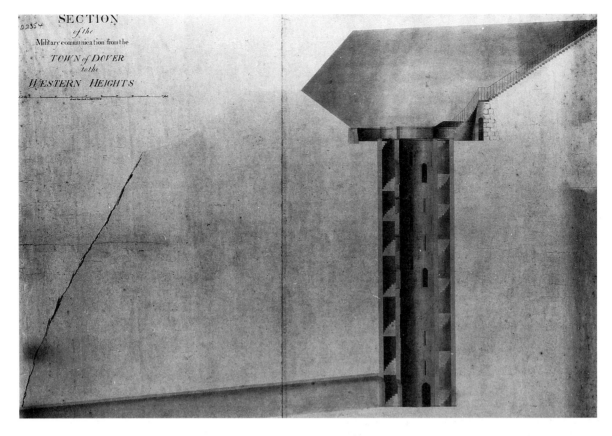

43 *A contemporary cross-section of Grand Shaft and its approach tunnel.*

By March 1805 Twiss had 480 men at work on Western Heights, the majority on the citadel and Drop Redoubt. Most of the preliminary work, after staking out the plans on the ground, involved immense excavations to create the ditches and form the ramparts and bastions. Over the next few years minor modifications were made to the original plans, but the fortress remains substantially that designed in 1804 by Captain William Ford under Twiss's supervision.

At the end of March 1805 it was reported that:

> ... the northern entrance of the southern Intrenchment ... is in a forward state, and one of the flanks has been advancd in order to command the approach thereto more perfectly ... The ditch of the gorge of the

44 *Looking up Grand Shaft after its restoration by Dover District Council.*

citadel has been deepened in many places and a wooden bridge has been made at the centre entrance to it ... The earth is nearly laid for the North Centre Bastion ... the roads of communication through the works are nearly all laid ... The scarp of the curtain to the Drop Redoubt has been considerably deepened. The parapet of the ditch in front of Drop Redoubt warrants about three feet ... The officers' barracks are in a pretty forward state ...

Work was plainly under way over the whole extent of the Western Heights (**45**). Across the Straits, visible on clear days to any Royal Engineer officers with spy glasses, French invasion preparations were also moving to a climax.

For Twiss, part of the early summer of 1805 was spent recovering from an illness, but by the end of July he was well enough to inspect the works. At Drop Redoubt, where the small

45 A pre-war aerial photograph of Western Heights Citadel. Much of the ditch of the western outworks has since been infilled and prison building occupy most of the old parade ground.

size of the fort made the troops more vulnerable to any concentrated bombardment, he proposed bomb-proof barracks for the 200 men of the garrison. He also advocated:

> ... casemated defences under the counterscarp for the defence of the ditches, between which defences and the interior of the works it will be very easy to make underground communications as the soil is chalk.

His suggestions for vaulted barracks were accepted, but the counterscarp galleries were never built (**46**). The existing caponiers, which are such conspicuous features of the redoubt, were added in the 1850s. By the end of 1806, the casemates, guard room and magazine were completed except for paving. There was however a set back in November when heavy rain damaged many of the new earthworks.

Just before Christmas 1805, Twiss was able to inform Morse that he had solved one of the major problems on Western Heights:

I have the honour to report to you that in sinking the well in the CITADEL ... we found water at the depth of 420 feet [128m] and that by having three reliefs of workmen and employing them day and night, we have got 20 feet [6m] deeper, which in my opinion will secure us about 25 feet [7.6m] of water when the springs are at the lowest, as at present, and nearly 40 feet [12m] of water for the greatest part of the year. I now recommend that the Board do immediately con-

tract for a simple machine to work with three buckets in this well, on the same principal as that I had constructed for the well in the cliff casemate in Dover Castle ...

This was a prodigious feat of engineering and absolutely crucial if a garrison was to occupy Western Heights for any length of time under siege. The well is a smaller version of the better-known Grand Shaft which was under construction at the same time. However, its central brick shaft has only two narrow staircases winding down round it for maintenance purposes.

46 *Drop Redoubt from the air in 1962. Prominent within the fort is the group of five casemated barracks. The caponiers in the moat were added in the early 1860s. Grand Shaft Barracks lie to the right.*

47 *One of the stairs leading down into the citadel casemates. The astonishing quality and massive strength of the brickwork is immediately apparent.*

Despite success with the well, for over two years the citadel was to cause Twiss major problems. These stemmed from it being the only part of Western Heights where significant progress had been made during the War of American Independence. Twiss in effect inherited a 20-year-old part-built fortification which, he felt, needed to be redesigned. Not least, he felt that the earthworks should be made much stronger by the addition of 18ft (5.5m) high brick revetment walls lining the ditches, and with small casemates or caponiers to defend re-entrant angles. In 1804, these proposals were rejected, not least on the grounds that to incorporate them would seriously weaken the citadel while the improvement works were in progress. With invasion thought to be imminent, such a

course was considered far too risky.

In March 1806, permission was given to complete the parapets, ditches, communications, lines, tanks and casemates of Drop Redoubt. The great ditch which was to run from the rear of the citadel to the edge of the cliff to the south was also authorised (**colour plate 13**). In the course of work that year, the engineers uncovered remains of the Knights' Templars' church on the hillside. These were carefully preserved and can still be seen. Once again, a request to revet the ditches of the citadel was refused. It was 'to remain as a field work without alteration for the present year'.

Nature however, took a hand. In the winter of 1805–6, heavy rain had caused the collapse of part of the banks of the citadel. In November 1806, a wet autumn led to another serious collapse here, in part prompted by altering the angle of the scarp slopes from 45 degrees to 60 degrees to make them more formidable to assailants. Brick revetments were seen as the only solution. Their expense, and the fact that their addition would turn the fieldworks of the citadel into a permanent fortification, delayed a decision until the following autumn. Then, a special committee of engineers, headed by Twiss, was asked to examine the whole design of the citadel. They reported that while it would be preferable to start again and lay out a new citadel to a more regular plan, in practice this was not possible. Instead, they recommended that 'the existing western front, as well as the flanks towards the north and south should be revetted, introducing casemated defences adapted to the figure of the work'. The acceptance of this report marked the turning point: Page's fieldworks were to be a permanent if somewhat irregular citadel (**47**).

By the summer of 1808, revised plans were well under way. The addition of brick revetment walls to the moats enabled the engineers to increase significantly the local defences by incorporating casemated galleries to give flanking fire along the ditches. By November 1809, work on the west front of the citadel was nearly finished. For the 1810 season, Twiss proposed to excavate the ditch along the gorge or rear of the citadel. He estimated that he would need 1200 workmen 'of such regiments as have been accustomed to breaking ground, including the Royal Cornish Miners who are most essential to our proceedings'. By August 1810 he hoped the excavations would be sufficently advanced to allow the revetting of:

> the scarp of the counterscarp on the south, which connects the Citadel with the range of casemates defending the entrenchments that fall on the sea cliffs; and to the northwards, the North Centre Bastion.

Construction of the three main magazines within the citadel could also begin, and it was estimated that a total of six million bricks and 130 bricklayers would be needed. Two million bricks were to be shipped from Grays in Essex and a million were to come from kilns near Dover.

As early as October 1804, Twiss had proposed a total of 139 heavy weapons for these fortifications. Most were to be 18 and 24pdr guns, but he included a substantial number of carronades, their heavy smashing power over short distances especially useful in protecting flanks and ditches during an assault. The decision in 1807 to incorporate casemates to provide flanking fire along the ditches prompted several experiments to decide the best design for their gun embrasures. Ford made the novel suggestion that they should be lined with cast iron, but in this, he was half-a-century ahead of his time. Trials with brick and stone embrasures of different designs took place over a number of months at the Chatham Lines and again in 1812, when Ford set up a butt in one of the Dover ditches to discover the best weapon for casemate use. The war was to end before many weapons could be installed; apparently only Drop Redoubt was reasonably armed.

By the begining of 1810, with nearly £137,000 spent, the Master General of Ordnance asked if

48 *Looking east along Western Heights to Drop Redoubt. This 1959 photograph shows the north entrance still in use, the earthworks beyond as yet unbreeched by the present road.*

the works could be stopped 'until a more favourable occasion may arise of proceeding with them'. By now, invasion was increasingly unlikely and the main theatre of war was on the Spanish peninsula, but half-completed works could not just be abandoned. Nevertheless, operations do seem to have been slowed a little. 1813 was the last year of heavy expenditure when just under £30,000 was spent. Ford, aware that the war might not last much longer, and conscious that peace would bring an immediate halt to operations, sought to complete the three distinct works: the Citadel, North Centre Bastion and Drop Redoubt. In this he was disappointed. In 1814 the Board of Ordnance halted virtually all works on the Heights. In 1815, expenditure dwindled to a little over £1000 and it ceased entirely in 1816. As yet unfinished were parts of the Citadel, North Centre Bastion and sections of the northern ditch and rampart

linking these to Drop Redoubt (**48**). Only the latter was complete, except for a ditch from the Drop to the cliff edge.

Ever optimistic, in 1814 and again in 1817 Ford proposed elaborate plans to link the castle with Western Heights by a massive entrenched work round the north of the town. Part of the castle itself was to be demolished and replaced by a system of advanced works. He estimated the whole scheme at around £230,000 plus an additional £90,000 to finish Western Heights. Not surprisingly, nothing ever came of this proposal.

Between 1804 and 1815, nearly £240,000 was spent on Western Heights. For the first time, both hills overlooking the harbour were heavily fortified, and for the first time since its completion, the castle was not the dominant defensive work. For the next century, castle and Western Heights were thought of together as the defences of Dover.

12

Nineteenth-century Dover

At the end of the Napoleonic wars, the defences of Dover were rapidly reduced. In December 1819, the Board of Ordnance ordered that the guns 'which are designated for works on the Western Heights should ... be withdrawn to the Royal Arsenal'. Much of the Heights were let for grazing and from then until the 1850s only spasmodic repairs and maintenance were carried out; Drop Redoubt alone retained a small garrison.

At the castle, the Coastal Blockade service, set up to combat smuggling gangs, used the cliff casemate barracks as their local headquarters until 1828, when they moved to more convenient accommodation next to Guilford Battery. Most of the buildings within the castle stood empty, although a small peacetime garrison remained. In 1834, it was proposed to let the interior for grazing. This, however, presented problems of safety. As the senior officer noted in a report, the area contained:

... scattered magazines, storehouses, entrances and openings to underground communications and extensive casemates, great and dangerous quantities of gunpowder, [and] various stores with ordnance shot and carriages ...

Furthermore, he wondered if:

... the policy of giving a legal right to any tenants and to their servants (of whatever character) to enter at pleasure a stronghold confided to the care of military officers should be adverted to ... at a time when the public mind is continually agitated by political clubs and societies.

In the wake of the Great Reform Bill, this was a powerful argument – used again by the War Office a century later when the Ancient Monuments Inspectorate was seeking to take control of the keep – and nothing came of the proposal.

But by the 1840s, concern was again being expressed about the security of Dover. Cross-Channel traffic was developing rapidly, spurred by the arrival of the railways and the development of steam ships. The latter, it was noted, could speedily transport large numbers of enemy troops across the Channel, irrespective of wind and tide. The Royal Navy might be the country's main defence, but in the context of Dover, proximity to the Continent suggested that it would be prudent to up-date the fortifications.

In 1841, the Master General of Ordnance was advocating a gun tower 'armed with one or two heavy guns' to keep ships at a distance. The Admiralty meanwhile in 1840 selected Dover Harbour to be a 'Harbour of Refuge', capable of 'receiving any class of vessels, under all circumstances of wind and tide'. In 1847 Admiralty Pier was begun on the western side of the bay to create sheltered moorings; by

1866 it was nearly 1500 ft (458m) long.

The better the harbour, the more essential it became to ensure its defence. In 1853, the Royal Engineers suggested a series of three-tier gun batteries at intervals on the Admiralty Pier. No designs survive for these, but the engineers probably envisaged something similar to Forts Albert and Victoria, then under construction on the Isle of Wight to protect the Needles Passage.

In the 1850s, the technology of warfare was being transformed. Steam-driven warships were threatening the Royal Navy's massive superiority in sailing warships, while developments in artillery were making existing defences obsolete. By the late 1850s, rifled guns were able to fire explosive shells accurately over

49 *The 1853 caponier providing a covered way to Hudson's Bastion from within the castle to the left, as well as additional fire-power along the eastern ditch. A 1982 photograph.*

8000 yards (7300m). Military committees, newspapers, and numerous pamphleteers warned of the dangerous consequences. The design of fortifications had to be rethought. As a committee of artillery officers noted in 1859, it was:

> … impossible for the Committee, in the very infancy of an invention which produces effects of so novel a character, to anticipate the changes which may take place in the attack or defence of works from the employment of these new cannon.

What was certain was that an enemy now had to be kept five miles (8km) from his target. The days of continuous lines of bastionned defences were over. Detached, polygonal forts, in range of each other for mutual protection, were seen as the solution.

At Dover, however, military engineers had to adapt the existing defences. In 1853, major

work began on modernising the castle. On the eastern side, the outer moat from Avranches Tower to the cliff edge was deepened and partly brick lined. A caponier was built across it to the rear of Hudson's Bastion (**49**). The main earthworks were all reprofiled and thickened to resist better the new explosive shells. Expense magazines were built at intervals on the main ramparts, and a new drawbridge was provided at Fitzwilliam Gateway. At the northern tip of the castle, counterscarp galleries were added to the rear of the redan to improve local defence. The further extension to the tunnels or countermines below the Deal road may have been part of this same campaign, as was the protective earth bank burying the southern side of the powder magazine at Canons Gateway (see **36**). Hitherto, bombardment from the sea had not been considered a serious threat to the castle. All these works in the mid 1850s were supervised by Captain Ben Hay Martindale, the senior Royal Engineer for the Dover district.

At both the castle and Western Heights there was an extensive programme to provide more accommodation for the army. Immediately outside Palace Gate was built a huge barracks which survived into the early 1960s (see **60**). Other smaller barracks were fitted in wherever there was space, most notably on the western side of the castle south of Colton's Gateway and Peverell's Gateway. As these were built before central messing, they were paralleled by a number of small detached kitchens. Meals produced in these were eaten in the individual barrack rooms. None of these detached kitchens survive, but opposite the former Debtors' Prison stands a small stone building erected in 1894 as a Bread and Meat Store, its overhanging roof shading the once-gauzed windows from the sun (**50**). The Debtors' Prison, out of use by the mid nineteenth century, was converted to Sergeants' Quarters in 1855. The most impressive result of this building campaign was the 'Officers' New Barracks' designed by Salvin and sited south of the *pharos*

50 *The late nineteenth-century bread and meat store; note the ventilated roof.*

overlooking the Channel (**51**). Measuring 383ft (117m) in length, it was constructed between December 1856 and June 1858 at a cost of £50,000. A contemporary guidebook noted that it held 45 officers, a mess establishment and had stabling for twelve horses and a coach house. 'It was first occupied in October 1858 by Colonel Gilpin and the officers of the Bedfordshire Militia.' It still stands, though most of its original interior has been removed.

By then, barracks space was at a premium, occasioned by the return of troops from the Crimean War in 1856. A contemporary observer recorded that:

At the close of the Crimean campaign, Dover was selected as one of the localities for the concentration of part of a division of the British Army. The limited barrack accommodation necessitated an encampment in the field, and no less than five regiments were tented on Western Heights. The troops became an object of great attraction and drew thousands of visitors to Dover.

The British Swiss Legion in 1856 no doubt considered themselves lucky to be billetted in the cliff casemates. Nearby, they would have seen further excavations. South of Canon's Gateway a spiral stairway of 214 steps was cut inside the cliff to link Moat's Bulwark and

51 *Salvin's 'Officers' New Barracks' of 1858 in the castle. The exterior remains largely unaltered. A photograph taken not long after completion.*

Guilford Battery to the castle. At intervals, defensible landings and doorways with firing slits were incorporated, while lighting passages led to openings in the cliff face. In the 1939–45 War, some of the latter were converted to observation posts and had short accommodation tunnels added to their rear. Guilford Battery itself had its parapets raised in 1853–4 and 42pdr guns installed on traversing mounts, while a certain amount of modernisation work was also undertaken on Moat's Bulwark.

The most curious part of the 1853 modernisation programme was the work on Henry II's inner bailey. Wall walk, towers and parapets were reconstructed into their present form 'for musketry', and Palace Gateway and King's Gateway were remodelled to their existing appearance and given new drawbridges. These 'were of so simple a construction that a few seconds suffice to either lower or raise them' (see **14**). The few remains of the medieval Well

Tower were finally swept away. It is clear that the military engineers were reviving the early medieval notion of 'keep of last resort' and anticipating that the garrison would retreat in a time of crisis to the inner bailey and keep, there to hold out until relieved. This thinking is exactly paralleled in the 'keep and bailey' design of the three contemporary forts then being built to form part of the Gosport Advanced Lines in Hampshire.

A significant phase in this reinvigoration of the castle was the restoration of St Mary-in-Castro (**52**). The state of the ruined church, last used as a coal store half-a-century before, was an increasing affront to the Victorian army. As barrack accommodation grew, there was also a practical need for a place of worship for the troops stationed there. In 1862, the architect Sir George Gilbert Scott undertook its restoration for use as the garrison church. He was fairly conservative in his approach compared to his successor William Butterfield. In 1888 the latter completed the crossing tower and added the vestry and the somewhat overwhelming mosaics which dominate the nave (see **3**). Despite all this, the church still retains much of its Anglo-Saxon work, which in turn reuses Roman brick and tile.

Nearby, something of an oasis in the midst of all the renascent military activity, was built a school house for the children of the garrison. This is now the church hall.

Along with the mid-Victorian concern for the spiritual welfare of the army went a continuing desire to improve the troops' living conditions. New barracks were one manifestation of this, improvements to the old were another. The Georgian barracks in Keep Yard were given improved heating and ventilation; later, small latrine blocks were added with some care for their surroundings (see **colour plate 8**). In 1868 substantial two-storey stone 'Canteen and Recreation Rooms', probably designed by a Royal Engineer Colonel I. A. Ross in a debased gothic style loosely modelled on Salvin's Officers' Mess, were built near Canon's Gateway (**53**). The building was well sited to tempt soldiers who might otherwise have headed for the taverns of the town below. By the early twentieth century, it incorporated a

library, reading rooms and a billiards room and had been renamed the Regimental Institute, one of hundreds of similar buildings to be found at army establishments throughout the empire.

The last accommodation to be reorganised was at Constable's Tower (see **19** and **20**). By the latter part of the nineteenth century, the Deputy Constable was a General commanding this south eastern military district. Existing quarters above the gateway were far too cramped and, between April 1883 and July 1884, the rear of the medieval work was extensively altered and extended back on both sides of the roadway. On the southern side an imposing new stairway and hall were added, together with a study. The original medieval great hall above the gateway was remodelled, while north of the gatepassage new kitchens and service rooms were provided. A separate coach house and stables with staff accommodation above were built to the north of Constable's Tower.

52 *The ruins of St Mary-in-Castro before the restoration begun in 1862. Note the* pharos *is linked to the church.*

53 The Canteen and Recreation Rooms, built in 1868, later renamed the Regimental Institute.

These additions were designed by R. Dawson Scott in a loose interpretation of Tudor gothic.

The mid-century modernisation works at the castle were paralleled by similar but more costly operations on Western Heights. In the area around the top of Grand Shaft, extra barracks were constructed; these were all swept away in the early 1960s (see **42**).

In 1853 work began on completing the citadel, left in an unfinished state in 1816. Estimates came to just under £12,000 for completing the ditches, revetting them and installing gun positions on the ramparts above. Opportunity was also taken to incorporate flanking casemates commanding the ditches, and in the South Lines to build huge two-storey casemates, apparently designed to hold 500 men. All this work seems to have been finished by late 1855.

Four years later, in 1859, another invasion scare gripped the country. A combination of incidents raised fears of a French attack on a Britain whose defences were widely thought to be inadequate. A Royal Commission was appointed, and although it concentrated on the defences of the great naval bases, it recognised that Dover was a special case, on account of its location and its strategic harbour. The secretary to the Commission, in a key position to influence its findings, was Major W.F.D. Jervois, the

Assistant Inspector-General of Fortifications. Both he and General Sir John Fox Burgoyne, his superior officer, had already studied Dover and made recommendations. It was a combination of their views which formed part of the Royal Commission report. In 1860, Parliament agreed that £165,000 should be spent securing Dover; the Royal Commission was to recommend that a further £170,000 be added to this figure.

Jervois' recommendations for Western Heights were fairly modest. At Drop Redoubt, he added powerful scarp galleries and two-tier caponiers, reforming the ditch around the latter (see **46**). The main powder magazine was mounded over for added protection. He also completed the ditch from the eastern side of Drop Redoubt to the cliff edge, extending the south east scarp galleries so they could fire directly down it. The North Lines, linking the

54 Western Heights. The entrance to the North Lines.

citadel to Drop Redoubt via North Centre Bastion, needed its ditch deepening and the chalk revetting (**54**). North Centre Bastion itself was further strengthened in similar fashion to Drop Redoubt.

Within the citadel, Jervois designed defensible quarters for the officers. This building was something of a tour de force, its loops and embrasures proclaiming its ultimate use as a keep-of-last-resort (**55**). More significantly, Jervois sought to remedy a serious military weakness in the actual citadel itself.

Military opinion was almost unanimous that an enemy attack on Western Heights would come along the high ground from the west. Page, Twiss, Ford and Morse had all tried to counter this by the great irregular bastionned trace of the citadel straddling the ridge, while North Centre Bastion dominated the valley to the north. However, as Jervois had correctly observed, there was still considerable dead

55 *The 1860 Officers' Mess in the Citadel. Like its counterpart in the castle, it enjoys magnificent views over the Straits of Dover.*

ground to the west. To dominate this, he drove a new ditch westward from the north demi-bastion along the northern scarp, and a second ditch north west from the south demi-bastion along the southern scarp. Some 200yds (180m) west of the citadel these were united in a powerful polygonal work. Guns on this covered the ridge ahead, while secondary armament provided enfilading fire along the new north and south ditches. The salient angle of this western outworks had an unusual double caponier covering the forward ditches. It seems probable that these works were completed by December 1867 (see **45**). This same building campaign probably also saw the construction of North Lines Right Battery of four 64pdr RMLs immediately to the west of Drop Redoubt. These were carefully sited to cover the valley and ground to the north.

The 1859 Royal Commission had also looked at Dover Castle. Acknowledging the fundamental weakness that higher ground lay to the north east, the Commission adopted General Sir John Burgoyne's solution of a new detached fortress on the crest. Castle Hill Fort, soon renamed Fort Burgoyne, was started in 1860 and was probably completed about five years later. As Jervois was to note in 1874, it had transformed the defences on the east side of Dover. 'So long as it is held, an attack is impracticable either upon the castle or along the northern front of the Western Heights.'

In plan, Fort Burgoyne mirrors contemporary Royal Commission forts on Portsdown Hill above Portsmouth. Its polygonal shape allowed its heavy armament to bring a concentrated fire on the most likely direction of attack. Haxo casemates protected the main flanking armament while the ditches had caponiers for local defence. At the salient angle, there was a double caponier of similar design to the one on the western outworks. Unusually, extending from the flanks of the fort were two defensible lines, the western one reaching almost to the Spur at the northern end of the castle. These terminated in small rectangular redoubts which provided a secondary shield to the rear of the fort (see **71**).

By December 1873, all the main landward defences of Dover had been completed at a cost of nearly £300,000, although it is unlikely that the new emplacements ever mounted more than a few of the weapons for which they were designed. Long before completion, the invasion scare which had prompted their con-

56 *Shot-Yard Battery in the castle in the 1870s, showing an RML on a traversing carriage. The rear entrance to the cliff casemates is in the right foreground.*

57 Admiralty Turret. The temporary crane is seen lifting the first of the two 80 ton guns from its pontoon on 8 December 1881.

struction had been forgotten. More important-ly, armament design was evolving so rapidly that it made little sense to mount guns which were often obsolete almost before they were installed.

To cover the seaward approachs to Dover, coastal batteries were augmented. Archcliffe Fort was given a battery of 9in Rifled Muzzle Loaders in the early 1870s. Between 1871 and 1874, emplacements for no less than 15 heavy guns were constructed at the castle. On the eastern side, East Demi-Bastion was given two new weapons, while on the cliff edge south of the military hospital, Hospital Battery was con-structed for six guns. West of it, Shot Yard Battery held a further two weapons (**56**). Immediately outside the castle to the west, Shoulder of Mutton Battery mounted another five.

To supply these new coastal batteries at the castle, a powder magazine was sited immedi-ately west of the Officers' Mess. In origin this probably dates from the Napoleonic Wars, but in 1888–9 it was extensively rebuilt and protected against shell fire by a new covering of concrete and asphalt. It was surrounded by earth banks. In 1925, additional earth and chalk were used to bury the magazine completely so as to form a level area to be used as a company parade ground.

Finally, in 1895 a battery for three 9.2in guns on seaward facing mounts was built immediately west of the citadel. Only two guns were installed. These were paralleled by a simi-lar installation east of the castle on Langdon cliff. Here, four 10in guns were originally pro-posed, but in the event, two 6in and three 9.2in guns were mounted. Together, these batteries contained the most powerful weapons ever deployed at Dover during peacetime.

While all these works were under way on the high ground, attention was concentrated at intervals on the immediate harbour defences. In 1897 work was to begin on the detached southern breakwater and on the eastern arm. When completed some ten years later, these created the Admiralty Harbour covering 247ha (610 acres). These still form the present boundaries of Dover harbour, their construction giving the Royal Navy the only secure anchorage between Sheerness and Portsmouth (see **71**).

Early proposals to build batteries and forts along the Admiralty Pier had come to nothing in the 1850s. But in 1867, Jervois, by now Director of Works for fortifications, again addressed the problem, emphasising that:

> When Dover Pier is completed, a small fort, which in conjunction with sea batteries on either flank of the existing work [Shoulder of Mutton Battery and Archcliffe Fort], would defend the harbour to seaward, should be placed at its extremity.

In 1872, work began; probably because of rapid developments in ordnance, progress was slow and it would not have been until 1876 at the earliest that the weapons were chosen. That year, the Italian warship *Duilio* was launched. Her twin 17.7in guns, each weighing 100 tons, made her the most powerful warship afloat. But in 1873 the British Admiralty had responded by ordering HMS *Inflexible*. Launched in 1881, she was armed with twin 16in Rifled Muzzle Loaders, the largest muzzle loaders ever installed in a Royal Navy warship. In 1875, proposals were made to mount similar guns in land-service turrets. Tests had shown that shells from such guns would penetrate 56in (1.4m) of iron and teak at 200 yards (183m). Probably at the instigation of Jervois, it was decided that Admiralty Pier should have a pair of these monster weapons.

Admiralty Pier thus ended not with a conventional fort, but with an armoured turret. As each gun barrel weighed 80 tons, steam power was essential for traversing the turret and elevating and loading the guns. These were the only steam-powered guns ever possessed by Coastal Artillery in Britain. The boilers, two engines, one of 30hp for loading, one of 300hp for powering the turret, together with their attendant stokers and engineers, were housed in well-protected chambers below the turret. Also down here were the magazines. A second cartridge room, situated below sea-level, was added in 1885. The circular turret itself had three seven inch layers of iron armour plate separated by two thinner layers of wrought-iron and teak. Turret and guns weighed 895 tons. The guns were installed at the end of 1881 (**57**) and when they were declared obsolete 20 years later, they were left in position. There they still remain, unique survivals of Victorian military technology.

By the 1890s, development of small, fast torpedo boats and destroyers had led to a demand for coastal defence weapons able to fire a large number of shells rapidly and accurately. These Quick Firing or QF guns ultimately made the heavier and more ponderous weapons of 20 years earlier obsolete. Nevertheless, for a time they existed side by side. By 1903, Archcliffe Fort had one 6pdr QF gun, and the original five weapons at Shoulder of Mutton Battery had been replaced by two QFs.

This growing arsenal of ever-more-complicated weapons demanded larger numbers of gunners. Many of these were trained reservists and what is now the castle restaurant was built in 1901 as a 'Mobilisation Store for Clothing, Arms and Accoutrements for 1000 Royal Garrison Artillery Reservists'. Amongst the accoutrements kept here were 1032 carbines.

13

A frontier fortress: twentieth-century Dover

Dover was to play a notable part in the two World Wars. Then, existing defences were augmented with a host of new weapons, from boom defences in the harbour to anti-aircraft and cross-Channel guns. It is not the purpose of this chapter to chronicle these wartime armaments in all their detail, but rather to look at the role of the castle and the permanent fortifications during this century of conflict.

In the years leading to the 1914–18 War, defences round the harbour were completed. The Admiralty Turret, abandoned around 1902, was replaced in 1909 by Pier Turret Battery, mounting two 6in guns. At the same time, the Eastern Arm was given three 12pdr weapons. Searchlight positions were built on the central breakwater, and when war broke out, these were augmented by a further battery of two 6in guns.

Within the castle, new barracks were built in 1912 just north of Canon's Gateway for the Royal Garrison Artillery (**58**). This had been founded in 1899 as a separate and distinct branch of the army specifically to man coastal defences. Its creation, however, probably meant very little change to the personnel in the castle, which had been mostly occupied since the early 1880s by coastal gunners. By the early years of the twentieth century, advances in fire control were enabling fortress commanders to exercise more centralised command of their gun batteries. In 1905, the obsolete Hospital Battery was converted to a fire command post.

On the cliff edge, overlooking harbour and Straits, it was superbly sited for controlling the guns round the harbour. In 1914, the Admiralty shifted its Port War Signal Station from Western Heights to new quarters built immediately above the Fire Command Post. From here, the navy was able to monitor and control all shipping entering and leaving the harbour. A wireless station was added to the rear, and when air-raids became a problem, a protective cover was installed in 1918 (**59**). The main naval headquarters however, remained down in the town.

When war was declared on 4 August 1914, the Royal Navy was already mobilised and at its war stations. Dover harbour was filling with destroyers and small craft; around it, the coastal guns were manned by the Royal Garrison Artillery. As the British Expeditionary Force crossed to France, the castle was witness to a new dimension in warfare which was to have profound consequences in a second great war a quarter of a century later. East of the castle, the flat grassland on the top of Langdon Cliff for three days that August became the springboard for the first four squadrons of the Royal Flying Corps to cross to Amiens to join the British army. It was only five years since Bleriot had become the first man to fly an aircraft across the Channel, landing on the hillside below Fitzwilliam Gateway. He had only just made land: the flimsy machines of the Royal Flying Corps had little more endurance

58 *The Royal Garrison Artillery barracks begun in 1912 opposite the Regimental Institute in the castle.*

and Langdon Cliff was the nearest possible point of take-off for France.

Later in the war, Dover was to be the target of air-raids. To counter these, anti-aircraft guns and searchlights were positioned round the town. One group of searchlights was located on Drop Redoubt, another on the roof of the keep. Within the castle, light anti-aircraft guns were placed near St Mary-in-Castro. By 1917, with food shortages increasing, vacant land round the church and elsewhere in the castle, was given over to vegetable gardens.

Throughout the war, the castle was mostly occupied by the Royal Garrison Artillery, but the keep found a different use. By 1900, the upper floors had been cleared, trophies of arms were displayed on the walls of the state apartments and the rooms were increasingly used for receptions and ceremonial occasions. On the outbreak of war, the keep became an armoury. Rifles, machine guns and other equipment were kept on tiers of racking and part of the space was devoted to an armourers' workshop. This use continued until the end of the 1920s.

Throughout the war, Dover was a key naval base, providing escorts for the troop and supply convoys to and from France. Although the main port for the army was to be established at Richborough, Dover was preferred for hospital ships which were able to berth alongside the ambulance trains in the new Marine Station. At the height of the Somme offensive in 1916, up to nine hospital ships arrived in one day. To protect ships against the growing menace of U-boats and torpedo craft operating from captured Belgian ports, the harbour was the headquarters of the Dover Patrol, which by 1917 numbered over 400 vessels. A busy naval dockyard, occupying the site of the present eastern car ferry terminal, serviced this fleet.

After the First World War, Dover resumed the peacetime life of a garrison town, with most troops quartered on Western Heights in the barracks round Grand Shaft. The actor David Niven, then a junior officer in the Highland Light Infantry, vividly recalled his first impressions, returning from Malta with his battalion early in the 1930s:

> We arrived in the Citadel Barracks, Dover, a few days before Christmas. It was a place of undiluted gloom. A grass-covered fortress, high in the mist above the slate-roof Victorian horror of the town below ...

In 1925, the Royal Garrison Artillery vacated the castle and from then until September 1939 it remained headquarters for 12 Infantry Brigade and for the Dover Garrison. Within the castle, the army continued to build, prompting the then Chief Inspector of Ancient Monuments, Sir Charles Peers, to comment in 1929 about 'the wretched designs of certain recent additions to the castle buildings' (**60**).

Further barracks were built in the 1930s outside the castle to the east. These, known as East Arrow Barracks, were demolished in the 1970s.

More serious damage to historic fabric was caused in 1938, when the army sited a new motor transport depot outside Fitzwilliam Gateway. The brick vault over the passageway crossing the ditch from Fitzwilliam Gateway was removed and replaced by the present brick parapets (see **colour plate 5**). This vault, which probably dated from the end of the eighteenth century, replaced a long-ruined medieval predecessor which had enabled the garrison to assemble unseen behind the outer gateway.

When war broke out in September 1939, Dover prepared to resume the role it had played a quarter of a century before. By then,

59 *Looking over the old Fire Command Post and port war signal station. The concrete roof was added in 1941.*

parts of the castle had been handed over to the Ancient Monuments Department of the Office of Works for display to visitors: these buildings were handed back 'for the duration'. The main coastal guns were reactivated and extra anti-aircraft defences were installed. Nobody thought that nine months later they would be facing the German army across the Straits.

After the Munich Crisis of 1938, when it became increasingly apparent that war with Hitler's Germany was inevitable, naval and military planners began looking round Dover for a secure headquarters for local commanders and their staffs. By 1938, the heavy bomber was adding a frightening new dimen-

60 *The castle shortly after the 1914–18 War showing many of the barracks since demolished. Long Gun Magazine can just be identified towards the bottom right. North of the castle is Connaught Barracks; to the north east, one of the flanking redoubts of Fort Burgoyne.*

sion to warfare. Fresh in everyone's minds was the carnage of the Spanish civil war, devastation which was to be augmented during September 1939 by the bombing of Warsaw and other Polish cities. The old Napoleonic tunnels, conveniently under the Port War Signal Station and impervious to bombing, were seen as the ideal location for such a headquarters (**61, 62**).

Proposals for the tunnels were drawn up in 1938. Initially, they envisaged the naval headquarters in the most easterly of the tunnels, with the Fortress Commander, the Coastal Artillery operations room and the anti-aircraft operations room located in the adjacent tunnels. Storage and dormitories took up the rest of the space. This plan was to be broadly followed until mid 1942, but changing requirements of the services lead to numerous modifications and dormitory accommodation was soon replaced by offices.

Just before the outbreak of war, the Admiralty appointed Vice-Admiral Bertram Ramsay as Flag Officer Dover, responsible for the Straits. It was to prove an inspired choice. Ramsay knew the area well for he had served in the Dover Patrol from 1915 to 1918, latterly in command of HMS *Broke*. That autumn, his naval staff moved in to the easternmost casemate. Here, the gaunt barrack room had been divided by timber partitions into numerous offices. At the seaward end of the tunnel, its windows giving Ramsay a view across to France on fine days, the admiral had his cabin or private quarters (**63**). Immediately behind

KEY

1 R.E. stores
2 Cookhouse
3 Well
4 Living accommodation
5 Commander 2AA Coy
6 Clerks' fixed defences
7 Commander and Adjutant's fixed defences
8 Telephone exchange
9 Fortress commander
10 Clerks' fortress headquarters
11 A.A. Commander
12 Gun operations room
13 Messengers
14 W/T office
15 Coding room
16 Writers
17 Operations room
18 Chief Staff Officer
19 Flag Lieutenant
20 Rear Admiral's cabin
21 Naval cipher coding office
22 Coding office

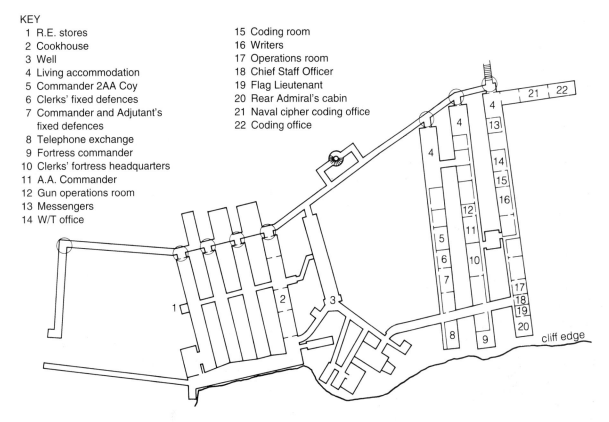

61 (Above) *The Underground Barracks ('Casemate level') in 1940.*

62 (Below) *A cross-section of the cliff tunnels as extended by 1943.*

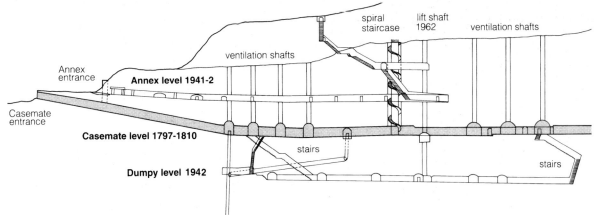

105

63 *Vice-Admiral Ramsay's cabin at the seaward end of Admiralty Casemate.*

were the Staff Officers' offices, then the Operations Room, where briefing meetings and conferences were held.

Much of the rest of the tunnel was devoted to communications, vital if the headquarters was to function effectively. The heart was the Wireless Office, flanked on one side by the coding room and later on the other by a teleprinter room. There was a constant flow of messages, information, orders and requests, from the Admiralty in London, from liason staff with the army and the Royal Air Force and from warships and other naval establishments. In a tiny room by the main cipher office, German-speaking personnel listened to enemy transmissions and, on occasion, sought

to confuse the Germans by broadcasting erroneous commands East of the castle on Langdon Cliffs, the brand-new lattice masts of the world's first radar chain contributed their knowledge of German air activity.

The wireless room was linked directly to the transmission mast above the Port War Signal Station, while the teleprinters and telephones used GPO land lines. For the first two years of the war, a naval telephone exchange operated in a tiny room in the next but one casemate overlooking the harbour. Within the castle pneumatic tubes centred on Canon's Gate guardroom carried messages between the tunnels, the keep, Officers' Mess and other main buildings.

Apart from Admiral Ramsay, who could sleep in his tunnel cabin when pressure of work did not allow him to leave his headquarters, there was no formal sleeping accommodation underground. W.R.N.S. and naval personnel were accommodated in requisitioned buildings in the town.

In the adjacent casemates were the Fortress Commander and his staff. Coastal artillery also established their operations room, and one was set up to control anti-aircraft defences and liaise closely with the Royal Air Force.

That first winter of the war, naval headquarters sought to ensure the safe passage of troops and supplies to France. Minefields were laid, boom defences were installed, anti-submarine and anti-torpedo boat patrols were organised and naval escorts were provided for the myriad vessels transporting and supplying the British Expeditionary Force.

But on 10 May 1940, the German army struck westward. Within three weeks, Holland and Belgium had surrendered and the German panzers had driven a wedge between the British and French armies. Ten days after the start of the *blitzkrieg*, as military disaster loomed, Ramsay began to assemble rescue ships and to evacuate non-combatants. The British Expeditionary Force, together with a substantial number of French troops, were trapped in a diminishing pocket of land centred on the port of Dunkirk. On 25 May, Boulogne was captured; the following day Calais fell.

By the evening of 26 May, Ramsay had collected 15 passenger ferries at Dover and a further 20 at Southampton. These it was thought could embark troops direct from quays at Dunkirk. To help in the evacuation, and to protect the merchant ships, Ramsay had a force of destroyers, corvettes, minesweepers and naval trawlers. Fast patrol boats were to engage marauding German E-boats. The main evacuation fleet was augmented by cargo vessels, coasters and some 40 Dutch self-propelled barges, known to the navy who manned them as 'skoots'. All ships of the British merchant marine had their regular civilian crews, both men and women. But as sheer exhaustion and the near-continuous shelling and bombing

began to take their toll, naval personnel had to be drafted in to help.

Behind this effort lay frantic round-the-clock work in the cliff tunnels. A naval staff-officer called it 'organised chaos'. Telephone calls to the Nore Command for further destroyers, telephone calls to the Ministry of Shipping for merchant ships, liason with the Southern Railway for special troop trains, calls to the Admiralty for tugs, weapons, ammunition, medical supplies, spare parts, fuel, rations and above all, trained men. The phone calls were endless. On 23 May Ramsay wrote to his wife: 'no bed for any of us last night, and probably not for many nights'. Two days later, he wrote again: 'days and nights are all one'. A little later: 'All my staff are completely worn out, yet I see no prospect of any let up.' Others in the Admiralty headquarters at this critical time recall exhausted personnel snatching a few minutes sleep stretched out on chairs or benches while work went on around them.

As the military situation deteriorated by the hour, naval plans repeatedly had to be changed, revised or abandoned. Instant decisions had to be made, frequently from confused and conflicting messages. Finally, in the early evening of 26 May, Ramsay received from the British government a formal signal to commence *Operation Dynamo*, the evacuation of the British army. At best, the Admiralty hoped that 45,000 troops might be saved in the two days before Dunkirk was expected to fall.

When the first ships of the rescue fleet arrived, they found the port ablaze and under heavy air-attack (**64**). Only two ferries, the *Royal Daffodil* and the *Canterbury*, succeeded in berthing and by the end of the first day, only 7500 troops had been rescued. It was clearly impossible to use the port.

At Dunkirk, Captain Tennant in charge of the naval shore party, signalled rescue vessels to be diverted to beaches east of the town. But here, shallow water meant that even at high tide, a destroyer could not approach within a mile of the shore. Troops had to be ferried out in ships' lifeboats and such small craft as could be found locally. Rescue was painfully slow. Faced with the prospect of saving only a tiny proportion of the army from the beaches, Captain Tennant decided to risk berthing ships alongside the spindly concrete-legged eastern mole with its narrow timber walkway which ran out nearly 1420 yards (1300m) from the eastern side of Dunkirk Harbour.

At 10.30 p.m. on the night of 27 May, Tennant ordered the *Queen of the Channel* alongside. Nine hundred and fifty men scrambled aboard, and though the ship was to be sunk on her way back to Dover, she had proved that the mole was usable. From then on, large ships headed for the mole while small craft operated off the beaches. Differences in loading speed were dramatic: HMS *Sabre* took two hours to load 100 men from the beach, but alongside the mole 500 troops boarded in 35 minutes.

In the casemates beneath Dover Castle, Ramsay was still asking for all available Royal Navy destroyers. More were sent from Portsmouth, others came from the Nore Command and the Western Approaches. The harbour was crowded with vessels unloading, taking on fresh supplies and heading back across the Straits (**65**). At peak periods, ships lay alongside the quays three or four deep. Many of the troops were wounded; the most urgent of these were operated on by medical teams on the quayside. In many cases, soldiers were given their first food for days before being put on special trains. In all, the Southern Railway provided some 327 troop trains from

64 *Dunkirk, oil tanks blazing; In the foreground, Royal Navy destroyers await their turn to evacuate troops.*

Dover during the nine days of the evacuation. The story was repeated at Folkestone, Margate and Ramsgate.

As soon as it had proved practical to use the mole at Dunkirk, the evacuation split into two distinct operations. The centre of events became the mole, to which Ramsay despatched successive convoys. Initially, these operated round the clock, but on 1 June so serious were losses from German bombing that it became necessary to operate largely at night.

The second theatre of operations was the eastern beaches. Here, only small craft could come close inshore. To supply these, the Admiralty put out an appeal for all readily available seaworthy pleasure craft. From the Thames, the Medway, east coast ports, the harbours and creeks of south east England, an armada of small craft manned by volunteer

65 *Evacuation vessels crowd Dover Harbour during Operation Dynamo. In the foreground French and British troops return on merchant ships while beyond lies a destroyer and in the distance Thames sailing barges.*

crews, many of whom had never sailed out of sight of land before, arrived at Sheerness Dockyard. Here, the navy checked the boats, issued fuel, rations and charts and organised them in convoys to Ramsgate for final sailing orders.

These pleasure craft were joined by a multitude of other ships: fishing smacks, lifeboats, trawlers, drifters, Thames sailing barges, the Leigh-on-Sea cockle boats, lifeboats from liners in port. Tugs were sent by the great towage companies – the docks at London, Newhaven, Portsmouth and Southampton were denuded.

Ramsay ordered the first convoy of 'little

ships' to sail from Ramsgate at 2200 hours in the evening of 29 May. By next day, they were streaming across the Channel in seemingly unending lines. The majority were heading for the beaches to act as tenders, but some of the larger vessels such as trawlers and drifters sailed directly for the port. On the bridge of the destroyer HMS *Malcolm*, returning from Dunkirk laden with troops, the sight reminded the First Lieutenant of the St Crispin's Day speech in *Henry V*:

> And Gentlemen of England, now abed,
> Shall think themselves accurs'd they were
>   not here.

Losses of ships, from bombing, mining and torpedoes mounted. Hard decisions had to be taken by Ramsay. On the night of 29 May, HMS *Wakeful*, laden with over 600 troops, was torpedoed and sank in 15 seconds. HMS *Grafton*, with 800 troops on board, was torpedoed as she stopped to rescue the few survivors. In the wake of this tragedy, Ramsay had to signal 'Vessels carrying troops not to stop to pick up survivors from ships sunk but are to inform other nearby ships'. Already that day, the Admiralty, alarmed by the number of damaged and sunk destroyers, had reluctantly withdrawn the eight newest and largest, well aware that they would be needed in future battles. But the destroyers and passenger ships were even more crucial in this battle, for only they had the carrying capacity to lift the numbers of troops. In desperation, on 30 May Ramsay telephoned the First Sea Lord and six of the eight were returned to him.

Heavy cloud on 30 May prevented German air attacks, but 1 June was fine and clear. By that evening, a total of 31 ships had been destroyed and eleven seriously damaged. Despite this, 65,000 troops were rescued that day. In America the *New York Times* wrote:

> So long as the English tongue survives, the word Dunkirk will be spoken with reverence.

In this harbour, such a hell on earth as never blazed before, at the end of a lost battle, the rags and blemishes that had hidden the soul of democracy fell away. There, beaten but unconquered, in shining splendour, she faced the enemy, this shining thing in the souls of free men which Hitler cannot command. It is the great tradition of democracy. It is a future. It is victory.

To the fighting men, to their rescuers and to the weary headquarters' staff beneath Dover Castle, such stirring and prophetic words might have been heartening if unbelievable. The evening of 2 June seemed likely to be the last time that Ramsay could send rescue ships before Dunkirk fell. That night, he despatched a force centred on 13 passenger ships, 14 minesweepers and 11 destroyers. At 2330 hours, Captain Tennant sent the historic signal from Dunkirk 'BEF evacuated'.

The following night one more evacuation proved possible. A force of British, French, Belgian and Dutch ships brought out 26,000 of the French rearguard. The next day, 4 June, the Prime Minister Winston Churchill was able to say to a packed House of Commons:

> When a week ago I asked the House to fix this afternoon for a statement, I feared it would be my hard lot to announce from this box the greatest military disaster in our long history.

Instead, he was able to tell of the 'miracle' of Dunkirk, the extraordinary evacuation, in which over 338,000 troops were brought back – the whole of the BEF at Dunkirk and 139,000 French soldiers. But Churchill warned his listeners:

> We must be very careful not to assign to this deliverance the attributes of a victory. Wars are not won by evacuations.

Nevertheless, the navy's success had an incalculable effect on morale. As Peter Fleming wrote later:

When it is remembered that *Operation Dynamo*, as originally conceived, had envisaged the evacuation over a period of two days of no more than 45,000 men, it will be seen how vastly the country's chances of survival had been improved by the Navy's resource and devotion. Throughout the rest of the summer British sea-power was to exert, mostly from a distance, a powerful influence on the German plans to conquer

the islands; but even before these plans took shape the Navy had given the nation two priceless assets with which to oppose them – an army, and a high heart.

The evacuation had succeeded beyond all expectations, although at a price. The army had had to leave behind all its heavy equipment; 693 British ships had taken part; 188 of the smaller craft had been sunk, as well as

66 *The Prime Minister, Winston Churchill, visiting Ramsay in his cliff headquarters.*

67 *A remarkable picture taken on 26 October 1941 from France showing German cross-Channel guns bombarding the radar towers east of the castle. The timber towers on the right have long been demolished; three of the metal ones on the left still stand.*

eight passenger ships, a hospital ship, trawlers, a sloop and six destroyers. Many others had been seriously damaged – out of more than 40 destroyers which had taken part, only 13 remained fit for immediate service. But behind this triumph lay the naval headquarters beneath Dover Castle. Had it not been for the organising genius, the leadership and drive of Vice-Admiral Ramsay here, the evacuation might never have achieved its extraordinary success. Certainly an author and journalist who himself manned one of the 'little ships' had no doubts, later writing:

> It is given to few men to command a miracle. It was so given to Bertram Home Ramsay, and the frail iron balcony that juts from the embrasure of the old casemate in the Dover cliff was the quarter deck from which he commanded one of the great campaigns in the sea story of Britain (**66**).

Three weeks after the Dunkirk evacuation, France surrendered. Dover was once again a frontier town facing imminent invasion. Once more, the northern French ports began to fill with invasion barges, but this time they were motorised or had tugs, and this time they were filled with the troops of the German *Wehrmacht* in their field grey rather than the more gaudy uniforms of Napoleon's Grand Army of 135 years before. Out in the Straits, British convoys were subjected to ferocious air attacks, the preliminary to the Battle of Britain, fought overhead from mid July to mid September 1940. For the next four years, Dover was to be the targets for German bombs and the shells of cross-Channel guns, earning this tip of Kent the title of Hellfire Corner (**67**).

In and around Dover defences sprouted. Barbed wire on the beaches, tank-traps and pill-boxes, many of which still remain, formed part of the national preparations. On Western Heights, St Martin's Battery was re-equipped with three 6in guns and in 1941 the lower end of the western ditch was fitted with petrol tanks and pumps as part of a Flame Barrage designed to protect sections of the coast by creating a wall of fire in the sea.

In the immediate aftermath of Dunkirk, the castle itself was provisioned to withstand a six-week siege in the event of invasion, and military engineers once again concentrated on strengthening its vulnerable northern end. A triple line of concrete tank traps was installed down the western side of the Spur to form part of a blockade of the road to Deal. Along both sides of the top of the spur itself were dug a series of slit trenches, those on the western side given added protection by a concrete wall or breastwork running back to the main ditch. This was overlooked by a new gun position cut through the medieval wall north of Treasurer's Tower. On the south eastern ramparts, anti-aircraft guns and searchlights were mounted. The old Fire Command Post on the cliff edge had a concrete blast wall erected behind it; a year later, in 1941, it was covered by the present reinforced concrete roof.

Outwardly, Dover Castle changed little in the course of the war, but beneath it a complete underground headquarters was to be created, safe from even the heaviest air attack. What in 1939 had been largely a naval headquarters in the old Napoleonic casemates, ultimately blossomed in 1943 into a Combined Headquarters for the main services (**68**). The navy was first joined here by coastal artillery, who established their headquarters in the tunnels adjacent to the Admiralty Casemate. Into these rooms information about activities in and above the Straits flowed from observers, pilots and warships, from intelligence gathering elsewhere, and from the new radar chain. Ultimately, gun batteries from North Foreland as far west as Hastings were controlled from here. By January 1941 the strength of coastal artillery in this sector numbered nearly 4500 troops.

By early 1941, pressure on the existing tunnels was such that a decision was taken to extend the system; three army tunnelling companies were brought in. An upper level of tunnels, forming a grid pattern, was begun a little to the west of the existing Napoleonic or 'Casemate' level. The new tunnels, named 'Annexe', initially were used as a hospital and dressing station, but later in part became dormitories. Compared to their Georgian predecessors in the Casemate barracks, service personnel billeted in these had considerably less space.

On Casemate level itself, extra communication equipment led to the excavation of a tunnel adjacent to the three eastern ones. This was used by the General Post Office for batteries and charging equipment for the telephone and teleprinter links. In the chalk between the Admiralty Casemate and the tunnel housing the coastal artillery headquarters, anti-aircraft operations and a new main telephone exchange, a passage was dug from the rear communications tunnel. This gave direct access to the operations rooms, bypassing the new telephone exchange (**69**).

The major excavation work late in 1941 was concentrated on digging, to the rear of Casemate level, a huge new Combined Headquarters for all three services. This was to have a central Operations Room while a grid of tunnels round it housed offices, communications equipment and other facilities. To avoid disturbing those working in Casemate level, a works tunnel was driven in from the eastern castle ditch. At the same time, work was also begun at the rear of Casemate level on a short

68 *ATS plotters at work in the coastal artillery operations room in the cliff casemates in 1942.*

69 *A reconstruction of the 1942 repeater station in the cliff casemates. This was a vital communication link between the castle and the rest of the country.*

tunnel to link this new headquarters – code-named Bastion Level. This new complex was part of the long-term planning for the invasion of northern Europe. It was one of three such command centres, one of which ultimately would be selected to control the invasion fleet and subsequent cross-Channel naval and military operations. But when approximately half of Bastion had been excavated, serious rock falls and subsidences forced the project to be abandoned. The Bastion tunnels have remained sealed ever since. Faced with this major set-back, a decision was taken in 1942 to excavate a further grid of tunnels some 50ft (16m) below Casemate level (**70**). This new level, codenamed Dumpy, was completed and

the Combined Headquarters were brought down here in the summer of 1943. However, the navy and coastal artillery, well-established in Casemate level and with a more narrowly focused role defending the Straits, retained their existing accommodation.

None of the primary planning for the 1944 Normandy landings was ever done at this Combined Headquarters, whose purpose was purely operational. Staff at the Dover CHQ were there to practise for their role in the invasion, and had the Pas de Calais been the chosen target, Dover would no doubt have been the operational CHQ. In the event, the Normandy beaches were selected and the honour went to the Portsmouth CHQ at Southwick House. It was entirely appropriate that Bertram Ramsay should be based there as supreme naval commander of the biggest invasion fleet in history. Just over four years from the day when he had completed the most extraordinary and successful evacuation of a beaten army, his meticulous preparations for an armada of 5298 vessels to put allied troops successfully ashore in northern France were under way. His old headquarters at Dover remained available in case Portsmouth was put out of action by enemy bombing, but with allied air superiority this was never a serious threat.

For the rest of the war, Dover headquarters continued to play an important role. Not the least of its tasks in the spring of 1944 had been to help generate spurious wireless traffic to deceive German forces into assuming that an allied invasion across the Straits was in preparation. There were ambitious plans to excavate further tunnels, but the war ended before much work had been undertaken.

With the end of the war in 1945, military activities in Dover were rapidly scaled down. Most of the barracks on Western Heights and

in the castle remained in use, but by the late 1950s their accommodation was becoming increasingly obsolete. The army withdrew to new barracks around Fort Burgoyne and at Shorncliffe. The Grand Shaft barracks on Western Heights were abandoned and demolished. Only the citadel found a new use as a prison for young offenders. In the 1950s, the castle itself had periods when no regiments were stationed in it – for a brief spell in late 1956 it housed Hungarian refugees who had fled after the Hungarian Uprising that autumn. Two years later, the first battalion of The Queen's Own Cameron Highlanders became the last unit to be quartered in the castle. When they departed in October 1958, only the continuing occupation of Constable's Tower by

70 *One of the staircases excavated in 1942 to link Casemate level with 'Dumpy' the new complex of tunnels 50ft (15m) below. These were later to be converted to a regional seat of government. They now stand largely empty.*

the Deputy Constable retained a direct link with the army which has probably been unbroken since 1066.

The wartime gun batteries were largely abandoned and in many cases dismantled soon after the end of hostilities. A few were retained on a care-and-maintenance basis, but in the era of the guided missile, they were seen as increasingly irrelevant. On 31 December 1956, the coastal artillery arm of the British army was abolished and the remaining batteries scrapped.

Within the castle tunnels, only the Royal Navy retained an interest. But in 1958 the Admiralty abandoned its headquarters here and that might have been the end of their use. But the same missiles and nuclear weapons, which had caused the demise of coastal artillery, led the Home Office to take the tunnels over to adapt them to form one of ten Regional Seats of Government in England. This was the time when the Cold War was at its height, there was widespread fear of Soviet intentions and of the 'three minute warning' of nuclear attack. In 1962, the Cuban missile crisis brought the world to the brink of nuclear war. Regional seats of Government, located in relatively secure accommodation, were intended to function after a nuclear attack which, it was assumed, would have destroyed London and the main machinery of government.

Under the threat of war, senior ministers would be appointed as Regional Commissioners with virtually unlimited powers to take charge of areas of the country. Aided by small teams of civilian and military advisors, in what remained of a post-Nuclear Britain their task would be to ensure law and order, to make the best and fairest use of remaining resources, to bury the dead and to try to maintain some of the machinery of government.

The Dover tunnels had been built during the era of conventional warfare. Throughout the 1960s and 1970s, to fit them for their new role the Home Office spent large sums of money, principally at Dumpy level. A lift was installed to link all three levels with the surface. The old spiral staircase was sealed at the top with a concrete cap as a precaution against nuclear contamination. Down below, new communications equipment, modern air-filtration plant and generators were installed. Space was found for large reserves of fuel, food and water. On Casemate level Ramsay's old headquarters, the local command centre for coastal artillery, the anti-aircraft operations room and the old telephone exchange were finally abandoned and their contents removed. The western group of tunnels, along with those at annexe level, were converted into dormitories and mess rooms. Then in 1984, the Home Office abandoned the tunnels after removing virtually all their equipment. Six years later, to commemorate the fiftieth anniversary of the Dunkirk evacuation, Casemate level was opened to visitors.

Epilogue

Dover Castle's long and stirring history, its remarkable architecture and complex defences, have made it one of the grandest historic sites in Britain. Antiquarian interest in the castle goes back to at least the sixteenth century, but it was not until the passing of the Ancient Monuments Protection Act in 1900 that active steps for its preservation could be taken by the Ancient Monuments Inspectorate. In 1898 the War Office had put a roof over the *pharos*, probably the first example here of wholly altruistic conservation work by that organisation. Colton's Gateway was similarly roofed a few years later, by which time the War Office was actively seeking to hand over what it regarded as the non-military parts of the castle. In 1904, St Mary-in-Castro, the *pharos* and Colton's Gateway were passed to the care of the Ancient Monuments Branch of the Ministry of Works. By 1908, Moat's Bulwark, Peverell's Tower and Constable's Tower had also been handed over – the last with the stipulation that it would remain the official residence of the Deputy Constable.

The 1914–18 War stopped further acquisitions, but in 1919 the Ministry of Works unsuccessfully sought to acquire Henry's great keep, then full of rifles and machine guns. A further request in March 1922 was similarly rejected, the Army Council no doubt mindful of the proximity of the Kent coalfield, attaching '… great importance … to the ability to make use of the keep for the storage of rifles etc in times of emergency, such as during the [miners'] strike last spring'.

Not until 1930 was the keep finally handed over. From 1932 to 1935 it underwent extensive repairs. The huge static water tanks on the roof and the roof of the chapel were dismantled. After considerable debate, and primarily for safety reasons, the keep battlements on the north and east sides were reinstated. These had been removed around 1800 to allow clear fields of fire for the roof-top guns. Avranches Tower was also conserved, while unemployment relief schemes allowed a certain amount of moat clearance and the regrading of some banks.

After the 1939–45 War, the process of transfer speeded up. Finally, in 1963 the remainder of the castle, except for the southern tunnels, was handed over for preservation. Since then, much has been achieved, but a great deal remains to be done. In such an exposed position, the 75 acres (30 ha) of earthworks and historic fabric need regular conservation. Brick and stone erodes, mortar joints need repointing; there is a constant battle against wet and dry rot in a castle built before the invention of damp-proof courses.

In the 1960s, growing recognition of the importance of the defences of Western Heights led to Drop Redoubt and North Centre Bastion being handed to the Ministry of Works for preservation. Archcliffe Fort, its seaward side removed in the 1920s by the Southern Railway was also acquired. More recently,

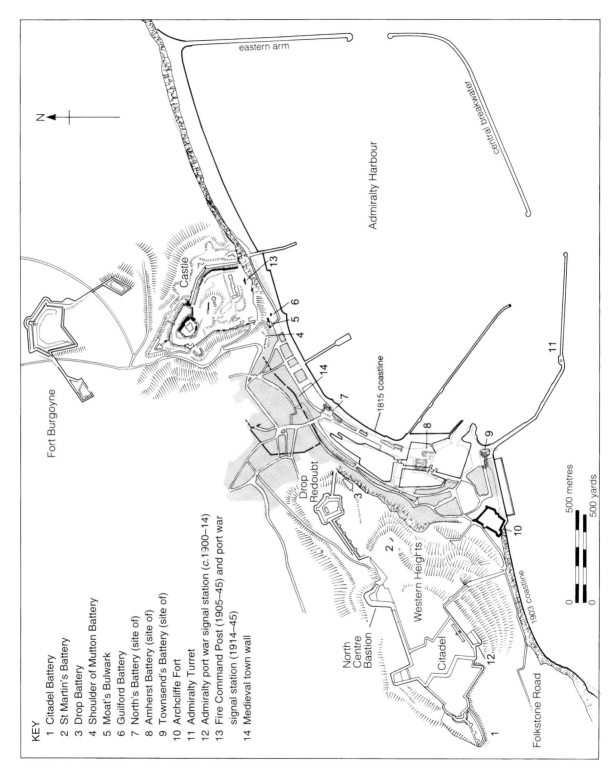

KEY

1 Citadel Battery
2 St Martin's Battery
3 Drop Battery
4 Shoulder of Mutton Battery
5 Moat's Bulwark
6 Guilford Battery
7 North's Battery (site of)
8 Amherst Battery (site of)
9 Townsend's Battery (site of)
10 Archcliffe Fort
11 Admiralty Turret
12 Admiralty port war signal station (c.1900–14)
13 Fire Command Post (1905–45) and port war
   signal station (1914–45)
14 Medieval town wall

71 *A location map of the Dover defences.*

Dover District Council has undertaken the conservation of the Grand Shaft and St Martin's Battery. Through its White Cliffs Countryside Project much of the derelict areas of Western Heights have been transformed. The site of Grand Shaft barracks, threatened for years with unsuitable development, has been declared a public open space.

Preservation of Dover Castle is assured; work has begun on conserving Drop Redoubt and plans are in hand for North Centre Bastion and Archcliffe Fort. The importance of the Dover turret is widely recogised. Yet, nearly 200 years after John Lyon bewailed the damage done 'by the demolishing hand of the modernising engineer', his successors might well feel that some things have not changed. In the 1960s, road engineers severed the northern lines of Western Heights for a comparatively lightly used road avoiding the monumental Northern Gateway. In the early 1990s, the A20 extension cut a devastating swathe through the southern flank of Western Heights, effectively destroying the southern barrier ditch, the Victorian coastal gun batteries and the Napoleonic outwork to Archcliffe Fort (see **24**). Had the fortifications of Western Heights remained as intact as those of the castle, the defences of Dover would have equalled those of many of the great frontier towns of western Europe. Even now, despite such damage, they yet remain among the finest in Britain, the castle unrivalled in grandeur and its position in history (**71**).

Glossary

Bailey Medieval fortified enclosure

Barbican Outwork protecting a gateway

Bastion Defencework projecting from main wall of fortress allowing garrison to fire along the latter

Battery A place where guns are positioned

Boom A floating barrier protecting a harbour mouth

Bulwark Early name for a small fort or blockhouse

Caponier A defensible covered passage across a dry ditch; sometimes also casemated to allow flanking fire along the ditch

Casemate Bombproof vaulted chamber, usually within a rampart. Occasionally with a gun embrasure, but often used for storage or barracks

Counterscarp Exterior face of a ditch

Counterscarp Gallery Passage within counterscarp with firing positions to defend ditch

Covered way Communication path on outer side of ditch protected from enemy fire by an earthwork parapet

Curtain Length of wall or rampart between wall towers or bastions forming main line of defence

Embrasure Opening through which a gun can be fired

Enfilade Fire sweeping along the length of a fortification

Expense magazine Small magazine close to gun battery containing immediately available ammunition

Flank Side of a defence work between the curtain and the face of a bastion

Gorge Rear of a defensive work

Motte A mound forming the defensive centre of an early castle

Redan An arrow-shaped outwork

Revetment A retaining wall for a rampart or ditch

Scarp Outer slope of a rampart or the inner side of a ditch

Terre-plein Surface of rampart where guns are mounted

Further reading

Dover has attracted the attention of writers for the last four hundred years. Among the numerous published works, the following have been found to be most useful:

Books

Andrews, C.B.(ed.) *Torrington Diaries 1781–1794*, London 1938

Bacon, Admiral Sir Reginald, *The Dover Patrol,* London 1919

Bloomfield, P. *Kent and the Napoleonic Wars*, Gloucester 1987 (ISBN 0 86299 340 7)

Colvin, H.M. (ed.) *The History of the King's Works*, Volumes 1 and 2, London 1963; Volume 3 (part 1), London 1975; Volume 4 (part 2), London 1982

Colvin, H.M. *Building Accounts of King Henry III*, Oxford 1971

Divine, D. *The Nine Days of Dunkirk*, London 1959

Fleming, P. *Invasion 1940*, London 1957

Firth, J.B. *Dover and the Great War*, Dover 1920

Glover, R. *Britain at Bay. Defence Against Bonaparte 1803–1814*, London 1973 (ISBN 0 04 940043 6)

Lord, W. *The Miracle of Dunkirk*, New York 1982

Lyon, J. *The History of the Town and Port of Dover and of Dover Castle*, Dover and London 1813–14

Murray, K.M.E. *Constitutional History of the Cinque Ports*, Manchester 1935

Naval Staff Monograph No 18: *The Dover Command Vol 1*, 1922

Niven, D. *The Moon's a Balloon*, London 1971 (ISBN 0 340 158174)

Plummer, R. *The Ships that Saved an Army*, Wellingborough 1990 (ISBN 1 85360 210 4)

Salzman, L.F. *Building in England down to 1540*, Oxford 1967

Scott, P. *The Battle of the Narrow Seas*, London 1945

Shenk, P. *Invasion of England 1940. The Planning of Operation Sealion*, London 1990 (ISBN 0 85177 548 9)

Statham, S.P.H. *The History of the Castle, Town and Port of Dover*, London 1899

Steer, F.W. *John Philipot's Roll of the Constables of Dover Castle and the Lord Wardens of the Cinque Ports 1627*, London 1956

Thurley, S. *The Royal Palaces of Tudor England*, Yale 1993 (ISBN 0 300 05420 3)

Turner, H.L. *Town Defences in England and Wales*, London 1970 (ISBN 0 212 98384 9)

Waugh, M. *Smuggling in Kent and Sussex 1700–1840*, Newbury 1985

Articles and booklets

Batcheller, W. *Descriptive Picture of Dover or The Visitor's New Guide*, undated but *c.*1862

Bennett, P. 'Dover Castle', *Canterbury's Archaeology,* 14th Annual Report 1989–90, Canterbury 1991

Brown, R.A. 'Royal Castle Building in England, 1154–1216', *English Historical Review* CCLXXVI, July 1955

Brown, R.A. *Dover Castle*, English Heritage 1974 (ISBN 85074 045 3)

Burridge, D. *The Dover Turret, Admiralty Pier Fort*, North Kent Books 1987 (ISBN 0 94830 502 9)

Coad J.G. and Lewis P.N. 'The Later Fortifications of Dover', *Post-Medieval Archaeology*, Vol 16, 1982

Coad, J.G. 'Dover Castle 1898–1963: Preservation of a Monument. A Postscript', Harper-Bill, C, Holdsworth, C. and Nelson, J.L. (eds) *Studies in Medieval History presented to R.Allen Brown*, Woodbridge 1989 (ISBN 0 85115 512 X)

Coad, J.G. *Dymchurch Martello Tower*, English Heritage 1990 (ISBN 1 85074 300 2)

Cook, A.M., Mynard, D.C. and Rigold, S.E., 'Excavations at Dover Castle, Principally in the Inner Ward', *J.B.A.A.* Third Series, Vol. XXXII 1969

Hardman, F.W. 'Castleguard Service of Dover Castle', *Arch.Cant.* XLIX, 1937

Renn, D.F. 'The Avranches Traverse At Dover Castle' *Arch.Cant.* LXXXIV, 1969

Reed. J. 'The Cross-Channel Guns', *After the Battle* No. 29, 1980 (ISSN 0306 154X)

Rigold, S.E. 'Excavations at Dover Castle 1964–1966', *J.B.A.A.* Third series Vol. XXX 1967

Wheeler, R.E.M. 'The Roman Lighthouse at Dover', *Arch.J.* 86, 1929

Wilkinson, D.P.R. *Historic Dover. An Archaeological Implications Survey of the Town*, Dover 1990

Primary source material

The following series of documents in the Public Record Office contain references to the construction of the cliff tunnels at the end of the eighteenth century: WO44 and WO55. Early plans are also here. WO166 and WO199 cover much of the later tunnels excavated in 1941–43.

The English Heritage Historic Plans Room also contains a valuable collection of plans of the Dover defences. These are mostly nineteenth- and twentieth-century.

Dover Museum has numerous illustrations and a valuable series of aural history transcripts recorded by civilians and service men and women who served in Dover in the 1939–45 War.

Index